# A Critical Black Pedagogy Reader

# About the Critical Black Pedagogy in Education Series

Series Editor: Abul Pitre

The Critical Black Pedagogy in Education Series highlights issues related to the education of Black students. The series offers a wide range of scholarly research that is thought-provoking and stimulating. It is designed to enhance the knowledge and skills of pre-service teachers, practicing teachers, administrators, school board members, and higher education employees as well as those concerned with the plight of Black education. A wide range of topics from K–12 and higher education are covered in the series relative to Black education. The series is theoretically driven by constructs found in cultural studies, critical pedagogy, multicultural education, critical race theory, and critical White studies. It is hoped that the series will generate renewed activism to uproot the social injustices that impact Black students.

## Titles in the Series

*Educating African American Students: Foundation, Curriculum, and Experiences*, edited by Abul Pitre, Esrom Pitre, Ruth Ray, and Twana Hilton-Pitre (2009)

*African American Women Educators: A Critical Examination of Their Pedagogies, Education Ideas, and Activism from the Nineteenth to the Mid-Twentieth Century*, edited by Karen A. Johnson, Abul Pitre, and Kenneth L. Johnson (2013)

*Multicultural Education for Educational Leaders: Critical Race Theory and Antiracist Perspectives*, by Abul Pitre, Tawannah Allen, and Esrom Pitre (2014)

*Educational Leadership and Louis Farrakhan*, by Abul Pitre (2017)

*Living the Legacy of African American Education: A Model for University and School Engagement*, edited by Sheryl L. Croft, Tiffany D. Pogue, and Vanessa Siddle Walker (2018)

*A Critical Black Pedagogy Reader: The Brothers Speak*, edited by Abul Pitre

# A Critical Black Pedagogy Reader

## *The Brothers Speak*

Edited by
Abul Pitre

ROWMAN & LITTLEFIELD
Lanham • Boulder • New York • London

Published by Rowman & Littlefield
An imprint of The Rowman & Littlefield Publishing Group, Inc.
4501 Forbes Boulevard, Suite 200, Lanham, Maryland 20706
www.rowman.com

6 Tinworth Street, London SE11 5AL

British Library Cataloguing in Publication Information Available

Library of Congress Control Number: 2019949386

# Contents

*Contents*

# Series Foreword

## Abul Pitre

*A Critical Black Pedagogy Reader: The Brothers Speak* is the first volume to capture this group of Black thought leaders and their critiques of education and society. Included in this volume are classic speeches and essays that address contemporary issues in the education of Black students. The book fills a gap in the critical pedagogy literature that has left out the voices of what might be considered the original critical pedagogues.

Critical pedagogy has been described as a framework that offers critique and empowerment to oppressed groups, thus this volume brings together a collection that covers the voices of leaders from 1852–1965. A careful review of the readings will lead one to see the impact that these speeches and essays have had on the development of the *Afrocentric Idea, Multicultural Education, Critical Pedagogy, Critical Race Theory*, and *Critical White Studies*, as well as other areas of educational discourse. This volume epitomizes the Critical Black Pedagogy in Education Series capturing and defining the key elements of the series.

The education of Black people has always been a concern for America's ruling elite causing them to spend millions of dollars crafting an educational agenda for Blacks in America. Historically, the state of Black education has been at the center of American life. When the first Blacks arrived in the Americas to be made slaves, a process of *mis-education* was systematized into the very fabric of American life. Newly arrived Blacks were dehumanized and forced through a process that has been described by a conspicuous slave owner named Willie Lynch as a "breaking process": "Hence the horse and the nigger must be broken; that is, break them from one form of mental life to another—keep the body and take the mind" (Hassan-EL, 2007, p. 14). This horrendous process of breaking Blacks from one form of mental life to another included an elaborate educational system that was designed to kill the creative Black mind.

Elijah Muhammad called this a process that made Black people blind, deaf, and dumb—meaning the minds of Black people were taken from them. He proclaimed, "Back when our fathers were brought here and put into slavery 400 years ago, 300 [of] which they served as servitude slaves, they taught our people everything against themselves" (Pitre, 2015, p. 12). Woodson (2008) similarly decried, "Even schools for Negroes, then, are places where they must be convinced of their inferiority. The thought of inferiority of the Negro is drilled into him in almost every class he enters and almost in every book he studies" (p. 2).

Today, Black education seems to be at a crossroads. With the passing of educational policies such as the *No Child Left Behind Act of 2001*, *Race to the Top*, and the *Every Student Succeeds Act* schools that serve a large majority of Black children have been under the scrutiny of politicians who vigilantly proclaim the need to improve schools while not realizing that these schools were never intended to educate or educe the divine powers within Black people. Watkins (2001) posits that after the Civil War, schools for Black people—particularly those in the South—were designed by wealthy philanthropists. These philanthropists designed "seventy-five years of education for blacks" (pp. 41–42). Seventy-five years from 1865 brings us to 1940, one has to consider the historical impact of seventy-five years of scripted education and its influence on the present state of Black education.

Presently, schools are still controlled by an elite ruling class who have the resources to shape educational policy (Spring, 2011). Woodson (2008) saw this as a problem in his day and argued, "The education of the Negroes, then, the most important thing in the uplift of Negroes, is almost entirely in the hands of those who have enslaved them and now segregate them" (p. 22). Here, Woodson cogently argues for historical understanding: "To point out merely the defects as they appear today will be of little benefit to the present and future generations. These things must be viewed in their historic setting. The conditions of today have been determined by what has taken place in the past" (p. 9). Watkins (2001) summarizes that the "white architects of black education . . . carefully selected and sponsored knowledge, which contributed to obedience, subservience, and political docility" (p. 40). Historical knowledge is essential to understanding the plight of Black education.

A major historical point in Black education was the famous *Brown v. the Board of Education Topeka Kansas*, in which the Supreme Court ruled that segregation deprived Blacks of educational equality. Thus, schools were ordered to integrate with all deliberate speed. This historic ruling has continued to impact the education of Black children in myriad and complex ways.

To date, the landmark case of *Brown v. the Board of Education Topeka Kansas* has not lived up to its stated purpose. A significant number of schools in the twenty-first century continue to be segregated. Even more dishearten-ing is that schools that are supposedly desegregated may have tracking pro-grams such as "gifted and talented" that attract White students and give schools the appearance of being integrated while being segregated within the school.

Spring (2006) calls this "second-generation segregation" and asserts: "Unlike segregation that existed by state laws in the South before the 1954 *Brown* decision, second generation forms of segregation can occur in schools with balanced racial populations; for instance, all White students may be placed in one academic track and all African American or Hispanic students in another track" (p. 82). In this type of setting, White supremacy may become rooted in the subconscious minds of both Black and White students. Nieto and Bode (2012) highlight the internalized damage that tracking may have on students when they say students "may begin to believe that their placement in these groups is natural and a true reflection of whether they are 'smart,' 'average,' or 'dumb'" (p. 111).

According to Oakes and Lipton (2007), "African American and Latino students are assigned to low-track classes more often than White (and Asian) students, leading to two separate schools in one building—one [W]hite and one minority" (p. 308). Nieto and Bode (2012) argue the teaching strategy in segregated settings "leaves its mark on pedagogy as well. Students in the lowest levels are most likely to be subjected to rote memorization and static teaching methods" (p. 111).

These findings are consistent with Lipman's (1998): "scholars have argued that desegregation policy has been framed by what is in the interest of [W]hites, has abstracted from excellence in education, and has been con-structed as racial integration, thus avoiding the central problem of institution-al racism" (p. 11). Hammond (2005) is not alone, then, in observing that "the school experiences of African American and other minority students in the United States continue to be substantially separate and unequal" (p. 202).

Clearly, the education of Black students must be addressed with a sense of urgency like never before. Lipman (1998) alludes to the crisis of Black education, noting that "The overwhelming failure of schools to develop the talents and potentials of students of color is a national crisis" (p. 2). In just about every negative category in education, Black children are overrepre-sented. Again Lipman (1998) alludes, "The character and depth of the crisis are only dimly depicted by low achievement scores and high rates of school failure and dropping out" (p. 2).

Under the guise of raising student achievement, the *No Child Left Behind Act* has instead contributed to the demise of educational equality for Black students. Hammond (2004) cites the negative impact of the law: "The Har-vard Civil Rights Project, along with other advocacy groups, has warned that the law threatens to increase the growing dropout rate and pushout rates for students of color, ultimately reducing access to education for these students rather than enhancing it" (p. 4).

Asante (2005) argues, "I cannot honestly say that I have ever found a school in the United States run by whites that adequately prepares black children to enter the world as sane human beings...an exploitative, capitalist system that enshrines plantation owners as saints and national heroes cannot possibly create sane black children" (p. 65). The education of Black students and its surrounding issues indeed makes for a national crisis that must be put at the forefront of the African American agenda for liberation.

There is a need for a wide range of scholars, educators, and activists to speak to the issues of educating Black students. In the past, significant scholarly research has been conducted on the education of Black students; however, there does not seem to be a coherent theoretical approach to addressing Black education. Thus, there is a need to examine Black leaders, scholars, activists, and their critique of the educational experiences of Black students. Critical Black Pedagogy in Education is one such approach that may offer an approach to addressing the educational challenges encountered by Black students. It is conceptually grounded in the educational philosophies of Elijah Muhammad, Carter G. Woodson, and others whose leadership and ideas could transform the educational experiences of Black students.

One can only imagine how schools would look if Elijah Muhammad, Carter G. Woodson, Marcus Garvey, or other significant Black leaders were leading educational institutions. Through the study of critical Black educators there is a possibility that an entirely new educational system could emerge. This new system should envision how Black leaders would transform schools within the context of our society's diversity. This would mean looking not only at historical Black leaders but also at contemporary extensions of these leaders.

Karen Johnson et al. (2014) describe the necessity for this perspective: "There is a need for researchers, educators, policy makers, etc. to comprehend the emancipatory teaching practices that African American teachers employed that in turn contributed to academic success of Black students as well as offered a vision for a more just society" (p. 99). Freire (2000) also lays a foundation for critical Black pedagogy in education by declaring, "it would be a contradiction in terms if the oppressors not only defended but actually implemented a liberating education" (p. 54).

*A Critical Black Pedagogy Reader* offers a philosophical foundation to begin eradicating inequities in schools and society. The critiques of these critical Black thinkers are the cornerstone of many of the cutting-edge theoretical frameworks that are being used to understand the educational crises impacting historically underserved students. Sadly, while these critical frameworks have origins in the work of critical Black thinkers, their voices have been virtually erased in the educational discourse. This volume seeks to rectify this omission by revisiting these classic speeches and essays that sparked social change in American society.

It is a welcome addition to the literature on Black education. Similar to Joyce King's (2005) *Black Education: A Transformative Research and Action Agenda for the New Century*, this book addresses research issues raised in *The Commission on Research in Black Education* (CORIBE). Like CORIBE's agenda, this book focuses on "using culture as an asset in the design of learning environments that are applicable to students' lives and that lead students toward more analytical and critical learning" (p. 353). The book is indeed provocative, compelling, and rich with information that will propel those concerned with equity, justice, and equality of education into a renewed activism.

## REFERENCES

Asante, K. (2005). *Race, rhetoric, & identity: The architecton of soul.* Amherst, NY: Humanity Books.

Freire, P. (2000). *Pedagogy of the oppressed.* New York: Continuum.

Hammond-Darling, L. (2004). From "separate but equal" to "no child left behind": The collision of new standards and old inequalities. In D. Meier and G. Wood (Eds.), *Many children left behind: How the no child left behind act is damaging our children and our schools* (pp. 3–32). Boston: Beacon Press.

———. (2005). New standards and old inequalities: School reform and the education of African American students. In J. King (Ed.), *Black education: A transformative research and action agenda for the new century* (pp. 197–224). Mahwah, NJ: Lawrence Erlbaum Associates.

Hassan-EL, K. (2007). *The Willie Lynch letter and the making of slaves.* Besenville, IL: Lushena Books.

Johnson, K., Pitre, A., & Johnson, K. (Eds.). (2014). *African American women educators: A critical examination of their pedagogies, educational ideas, and activism from the nineteenth to the mid-twentieth centuries.* Lanham, MD: Rowman & Littlefield Education.

King, J. E. (Ed.). (2005). *Black education: A transformative research and action agenda for the new century.* Mahwah, NJ: Lawrence Erlbaum Associates.

Lipman, P. (1998). *Race and the restructuring of school.* Albany, NY: SUNY Press.

Nieto, S., & Bode, P. (2012). *Affirming Diversity: The sociopolitical context of multicultural education* (6th ed.) Boston, MA: Allyn and Bacon.

Oakes, J., and Lipton, M. (2007). *Teaching to change the world* (3rd ed.). Boston, MA: McGraw Hill.

Pitre, A. (2015). *The education philosophy of Elijah Muhammad: Education for a new world* (3rd ed.). Lanham, MD: University Press of America.

Spring, J. (2006). *American education.* New York: McGraw Hill.

———. (2011). *The politics of American education.* New York: Routledge.

Watkins, W. (2001). *The white architects of black education: Ideology and power in America 1865–1954.* New York: Teachers College Press.

Woodson, C. G. (2008). *The mis-education of the Negro.* Drewryville, VA: Kha Books.

# Foreword

There are times in history when certain books must be written! *A Critical Black Pedagogy Reader: The Brothers Speak* is one of these books! The famous words of W.E.B. DuBois (1903) are still relevant today where he noted, "how does it feel to be a problem?" Given the current state of our nation's political and educational climate, Black students in our nation's educational system have been relegated to a substandard system where they have garnered media attention and a national spotlight not for the positive attributes they bring to the educational setting but for negative stories and headlines that are oftentimes manufactured to get likes and clicks.

I want to be crystal clear. Many Black students are facing an academic death in our nation's K–12 public, charter and private schools. Unfortunately, educators continue to make excuses why it is not their fault that Black students are not achieving academically. However, they never discuss what is in their power to change when Black students enter schools and school districts across this great nation. As a result, this book is a welcome addition to the education knowledge base as it provides a new and fresh perspective on how to effectively serve Black students.

It is my hope that this book reaches the educators and other stakeholders that it needs to reach to make a positive difference for Black students to achieve academically in the most affluent country in the world. We can no longer, in this age of educational accountability, continue to stand by and watch the achievement levels of this student population be at or near the bottom of every major academic barometer and be comfortable with our work as education professionals. Once the education profession chooses to fully embrace the educational potential of Black students, we will see transformation happen for Black students that want to achieve at a high level but are in schooling environments that do not develop their full potential.

This book, *A Critical Black Pedagogy Reader: The Brothers Speak* is also for Black parents who send their children to school expecting something great to happen only to be met with disappointment at the door of the school building. The greatness they expect for their Black children is why many work one, two or even three jobs to make sure their children have food on the table and a roof over their head just so they can make it to school! Unfortunately, when their Black child(ren) matriculate through our nation's schools, they are met with 'educational rhetoric.' This educational rhetoric tells the parents all that is perceived to be wrong with their child(ren) rather than how the schooling experience will put them in the best position to have a positive impact on their lives.

Finally, this book embraces the voices, hopes and dreams of so many who have died for Black students to have a right to a quality education in this country. We thank you for making the ultimate sacrifice so that one day the education profession can reach its full potential by serving the educational needs of Black students. I have come to learn that we have to continue to push until this change happens. This is why I commend Dr. Abul Pitre for this valuable contribution to the education profession. An intentional focus on Critical Black Pedagogy is exactly what we need at this moment. It is my hope that this book will spark a new movement of Black academic success!

Chance W. Lewis, PhD
Carol Grotnes Belk Distinguished Professor of Urban Education
Director, The Urban Education Collaborative
Provost Faculty Fellow for Diversity, Inclusion and Access
University of North Carolina at Charlotte

## REFERENCES

DuBois, W.E.B. (1903). *The souls of Black folk.* New York: Random House.

# Introduction

In the field of education, issues of diversity and social justice have emerged to become major areas of discourse. Included in the discourse on social justice are constructs in critical pedagogy. Critical pedagogy is a philosophy of education that emphasizes teaching students how to think critically about societal and even personal problems, understanding how structures of power and racism degrade the opportunities for democracy, economic justice, and personal development. It is a cornerstone of multicultural education (Nieto & Bode, 2018).

Although many educational theorists attribute the popularization of critical pedagogy to Paulo Freire and his 1968 book, *Pedagogy of the Oppressed*, the new wave of educational discourse regarding issues of diversity, equity, and social justice has roots in the writings and philosophy of critical black educators (Darder, Baltodano, & Torres, 2017). In the 1960s, high school and college campuses became the "terrain of struggle" as Black student protest disrupted business as usual (Pitre, 2011). Prior to the 1960s the consciousness of Black students had been raised by an array of Black leaders who offered a potent critique of society.

For example, a cornerstone of critical theory is questioning the neutrality of the knowledge being taught in schools; however, this very question had long been raised by critical Black educators (Apple, 2019; Au, 2012; McLaren, 2015; Pitre, 2011). James Banks (1992), in his article "African American Scholarship and the Evolution of Multicultural Education," writes that multicultural education has roots in the scholarship of Black scholars such as W. E. B. DuBois and Carter G. Woodson. These scholars and leaders offered an alternative perspective to the Eurocentric ideas that prevailed in education. They critiqued the educational systems that originated from their oppressors. And they understood that education was connected to liberation. The contributors to William Watkins's (2005) edited book, *Black Protest Thought and Education*, highlight some of the organizations and leaders who sought to use education as the engine for Black liberation.

Today the black struggle for equity in education has morphed into critiques of education that intersect with race, social class, religion, gender, sexual orientation, and special needs. New theoretical frameworks such as critical race theory and critical White studies have emerged to become leading areas of discourse among educators. At major conferences the themes reflect issues of diversity and social justice. A perusal of the American Education Research Association conference themes over the last several years demonstrates this new wave of educational discourse (AERA, n.d.; Cochrane, 2017). Conference presentations and book signings highlight the ideas of critical educators, multicultural scholars, and educators for social justice.

Icons of critical pedagogy rightfully receive volumes of accolades at these conferences. Some examples of this are the Paulo Freire special interest group of the AERA and the panels devoted to the Frankfurt School, one of the first group of European scholars who offered a critique of society and sought to dismantle oppressive and antidemocratic structures. The term *critical pedagogy* itself was first coined by Henry Giroux in his book, *Theory and Resistance in Education* (1985/2001). Darder, Torres, and Baltodano (2017) write, "Critical pedagogy is fundamentally committed to the development and enactment of a culture of schooling that supports the empowerment of culturally marginalized and economically disenfranchised students" (p. 10).

These developments show that the time is ripe for a broader consideration of the education of Black people in America in light of the principles of critical pedagogy, both those espoused by scholars like Freire, Giroux, and the Frankfurt school as well as those developed by Black scholars who preceded and followed them. Naim Akbar (2009) points out that the struggle for education for Black people began when the first Blacks were brought to America to be made slaves. Enslaved Blacks were severed completely from their culture, language, and religion, prohibited from reading (Spring, 2016), and often from speaking in their native languages. These brutal realities led to what Watkins (2005) describes as "nearly 400 years of protest" (p. 1).

These protests continue today in (among other efforts) the struggle to prepare educators for the growing diversity that exists in public schools by offering undergraduate and graduate courses on critical pedagogy. And a struggle it is: In the foundation courses, some of the required textbooks scantly cover Paulo Freire's chapter on "Banking Education." And while some textbooks may mention Du Bois and Woodson, they are largely silent on the many Black critical educators who have contributed to the development of critical pedagogy. This limitation is even more pronounced when it comes to critical race theory evolving from Black nationalist ideology. As

James Anderson (2005) writes, "scant attention has been paid to the place of education within the Black radical tradition" (ix).

Some of these underrepresented figures include Malcolm X who influenced Derrick Bell, one of the chief architects of critical race theory in the 1980s, and Elijah Muhammad, who wrote about education from a critical race perspective as far back as the 1960s. In 1995, Gloria Ladson-Billings and William Tate (1995) wrote the seminal article "Toward a Critical Race Theory of Education," in which they situated critical race theory in the context of education. The article highlighted three central propositions of critical race theory: that "race continues to be significant," that "U.S. society is based on property rights," and that "the intersection of race and property creates an analytic tool through which we can understand social (and consequently school) inequity" (p. 48). All of these propositions can be found in Elijah Muhammad's (1965) book, *Message to the Black Man in America,* in which he discusses landownership, citizenship, economics, and education.

The struggle to incorporate critical pedagogy into teacher training at colleges and postgraduate departments is, perhaps surprisingly, most pronounced at historically Black colleges and universities. However, teacher education programs in general often lack in-depth literature from critical Black educators, making it appear as though Black people had nothing to offer in terms of their own education. Most often in critical pedagogy textbooks, critical Black educators may be mentioned in a sidebar or bibliography, but they are rarely given center stage. Ricky Allen (2006) speaking to the absence of Blacks in the critical pedagogy discourse writes, "I would say that critical pedagogists, consciously or not, have been somewhat dismissive of all of those groups that Eduardo Bonilla-Silva (2006) defines as the "collective Black," or those who are treated as if they were Black" (p. 5).

This volume seeks to fill this gap in the literature by offering an anthology of writings that falls under the category of critical Black pedagogy. Coined in 2008, the term *critical Black pedagogy* is based on the educational theories of Carter Woodson and Elijah Muhammad and first appeared in the book *The Struggle for Black History: Foundations for a Critical Black Pedagogy in Education* (Pitre, 2008). The initial ideas from this book gave way to a book series titled "Critical Black Pedagogy in Education," upon which this volume is intended to build. In the course of this series, the four components of critical Black pedagogy were explored—Afrocentricity, multicultural education, critical pedagogy, and African American spirituality:

1. **Afrocentricity** is a frame of reference wherein phenomena are viewed from the perspective of African descended people. This approach is defined by Molefi Asante (1991) wherein he writes, "Afrocentricity is a frame of reference wherein phenomena are viewed from the perspective of the African person. The Afrocentric approach seeks in every

situation the appropriate centrality of the African person. In education this means that teachers provide students the opportunity to study the world and its people, concepts, and history from an African world view" (p. 171). It means that we must include an examination of Black leaders, scholars, students, and activists and their critique of Black education.

2. **Multicultural education** is a process of comprehensive school reform and basic education for students. It challenges and rejects racism and other forms of discrimination in schools and society and accepts and affirms pluralism (ethnic, racial, linguistic, religious, economic, and gender, among others) that students, their communities, and teachers reflect (Nieto & Bode, 2018). And it offers a praxis for addressing contemporary concerns related to Black education.

3. **Critical pedagogy** asks how and why knowledge gets constructed the way it does, and how and why some constructions of reality are legitimated and celebrated by the dominant culture while others are clearly not (McLaren, 2015, p. 133). And in the context of critical black pedagogy it asks a central question: What would schools and universities look like if Martin Luther King Jr. or Malcolm X were in leadership roles such as superintendent, principal, university president, provost, or chancellor?

4. **African American spirituality** posits that the African concept of life and its concept of education require that the sacred and the secular should be seen as one. The African worldview does not approach the study of God as some kind of force independent of the human reason and physical reality. Instead, it sees God as an inescapable component of human life (Akbar, 1998, p. 50).

In 2016, the first dissertation to use critical Black pedagogy as theoretical framework was produced by Jasmine Williams. Williams (2016) conducted a case study on Black homeschooling with a family who were members of the Nation of Islam. Using critical Black pedagogy as theoretical lens the study disclosed the powerful agency that Black people can have over their own education.

Critical Black pedagogy—and this volume in particular—seeks to restore the voices of Black thinkers into the study of critical pedagogy. Most prominent among those voices are Carter G. Woodson and Elijah Muhammad. Although Woodson's and Muhammad's writings are presented in more detail in the chapters that follow, it is worth previewing their contributions to critical Black pedagogy because of their outsized influence.

Woodson received his doctorate degree from Harvard University in 1912 and went on to become a leading scholar on Black education. Widely known as the father of Black history, Woodson's scholarship paved the way for many of the contemporary analyses of education. His critique of education speaks to core challenges of Black education in the twenty-first century: "The education of the Negroes, the most important thing in the uplift of the Negroes, is almost entirely in the hands of those who have enslaved and now segregate them" (Woodson, 1933, p. 20). An Afrocentric approach is absent from history courses, and Black students are subtly taught that their blackness is a curse. The idea of their own inferiority is drilled into the psyche of Black students, while White students are taught that they are superior to other people.

This is evident in "second-generation segregation"—meaning segregation *within* schools, creating two tracks, two schools in effect, in the same building (Spring, 2011). For example, you could have a school where the total population of Black students is 90% but they are only 2% percent of the students in honors or Advanced Placement classes. Woodson also pointed out that teacher education programs produced Black teachers who, while having more empathy for Black students, were being taught to view the world from a Eurocentric lens, making them figureheads: "The present system under the control of whites trains the Negro to be white. . . . Taught from books of the same bias, trained by Caucasians of the same prejudices or by Negroes of enslaved minds, one generation of Negro teachers after another have served no higher purpose than to do what they are told" (Woodson, 1933, p. 20).

This predated Paulo Freire's (1968) writings that argue that an exorcism must occur whereby the oppressed must overthrow the "oppressor consciousness" that has been lodged in their psyche: "Self-depreciation is another characteristic of the oppressed, which derives from their internalization of the opinion the oppressors hold of them. So often they hear that they are good for nothing know nothing and are incapable of learning anything—that they are sick, lazy, and unproductive—that in the end they become convinced of their own unfitness" (p. 63).

Woodson's powerful critique was a forerunner to what has been described as critical pedagogy. Darder et al. (2017) confirms Woodson's contributions to critical pedagogy writing, "The works of W. E. B. DuBois and Carter G. Woodson, often referred to as the father of Black History, rightly merit recognition for their important contributions to the evolution of critical pedagogical thought" (p. 3). Woodson's critiques of Black education are just as pertinent today as they were in the early 1900s, and his contributions continue to offer a light on educational inequities and mis-education.

Elijah Muhammad is another underappreciated early thinker regarding critical Black pedagogy. Numerous writers have written biographies of Muhammad but virtually nothing has been written about his thinking regarding Black education (Essein-Udom, 1962; Lincoln, 1994; Berg, 2009; Clegg, 2014). Elijah Muhammad grew up in the brutal environment of the Deep

South and eventually moved north to Detroit (Clegg, 2014). He struggled with work and drinking until he met with an itinerant *master teacher* called Prophet Fard who introduced him to Islam (J. Muhammad, 2009). His life took a dramatic turn, and he worked his way into leadership of the Black Islamic community that Fard had nurtured.

Along the way, he became particularly interested in Black education. He offered a critique of education that began with theology. Unlike educational theorists who might begin their critique of schools and the society, he starts his critique with the question: Who is God? His critique challenged the common belief that God and all his prophets and messengers were White men.

An entire curriculum was developed by Elijah Muhammad that became the basis for membership in the Nation of Islam, emphasizing the knowledge that is important to Black people rather than the select knowledge that White educational leaders would select for Black students. His critical pedagogy was an inspiration for many other figures who brought consciousness of racist ideology to the wider community, including Malcolm X, Louis Farrakhan, and Muhammad Ali (Pitre, 2010, 2015, 2017, 2018).

Derek Bell's (1992) "fourth rule" explains how some Black leaders are cast as radicals when their teaching becomes too threatening to the White majority. The fourth rule applies when a Black person or group makes a statement that the White community views as offensive. Those in power then seek to recruit Blacks to make a statement of denunciation of the Black person or group who has made the statement. Bell (1992) writes, "Those blacks who refuse to be recruited will be interpreted as endorsing the statements and action and may suffer political or economic reprisals" (p. 118). This has certainly applied to Black leaders who have vigorously critiqued the White educational establishment.

## ORGANIZATION OF THE READER

*A Critical Black Pedagogy Reader* brings together classic essays and speeches from Black leaders that speak to criticality in Black education. The anthology contains selections that are grouped according to the years they were published and is limited to selections from Black men. This decision was made to dispel negative stereotypes that have haunted this population and to provide a foundation for rethinking educational justice in the twenty-first century. It is also a response to the White male dominance in education that has rendered Black men voiceless in the critical educational discourse (Orelus & Brock, 2015).

This volume seeks to show that Black men were early advocates of a critical pedagogy and who knew that a White-controlled educational system would limit their opportunities for freedom. It illustrates that Black men have clapped back at the educational inequities experienced by historically underserved populations. In consonance with others who fought for social justice, Black men spoke and continue to speak to the inequities in education and society. And while the book is focused on the voices of Black men, it is not intended to place those oriented toward equity and social justice at opposite ends based on phenotype. It only offers an opportunity to revisit the critiques of a population that has been nearly muted in the critical pedagogy discourse.

The book is organized chronologically, capturing what Black male educators have said in their fight for equal justice. Each chapter specifically speaks to education with the exception of the first chapter by Frederick Douglass whose critique of the Fourth of July has implications for critical education theory. Many of these figures have been underrepresented in the academy, a situation that still plagues Black scholars today (Darder et al., 2017). To truly disrupt inequality in education aspiring and practicing educators need to study the voices of those who have been *locked in the margins* of the oppressive superstructure.

## Chapter 1

Chapter 1 presents a speech given by Frederick Douglass in 1852 titled "What to the Slave Is the Fourth of July?" This speech, while not focused on education per se, is an early example of Black thinkers offering a critique and counternarrative to the rhetoric of freedom and equality as it related to the Black experience in America (representing Reiland Rabaka's 2008 concept of Africana critical theory long before the Frankfurt School in the 1930s). The speech itself was a kind of critical pedagogy, seeking to educate readers on the hypocrisy of American idealism, arguing, "The power is co-extensive with the Star Spangled Banner and American Christianity. Where these go, may also go the merciless slave-hunter."

## Chapter 2

Chapter 2 presents Booker T. Washington's 1896 article for *The Atlantic,* "The Awakening of the Negro." Washington has been viewed by some as an accommodationist who steered Blacks toward a strictly industrial education. However, a closer reading of this article reveals his critical perspective—that Black economic power is a necessary driver of freedom.

His Tuskegee Institute trained students in farming, land management, and other skills that would allow them to be self-sufficient and escape the racist economic structures currently in place, structures that took the fruits of their labor as rents and that treated them as units of labor rather than as possible innovators and inventors. He recognized, along with others, that their oppressors would not simply give up power. Instead, he believed Blacks would gain freedom and self-determination when they had economic power, when they produced goods "that the white man wants or respects in the commercial world," when a "black man gets a mortgage on a white man's house that he can foreclose at will." For Washington, education should not support the status quo or simply supply White business owners with labor—it should produce Black creators and business owners who will transform the economic landscape.

## Chapter 3

In chapter 3, W. E. B. Du Bois, in his essay "The Education of Black Folk," points out how the schooling of Blacks has been designed to serve the needs of the owners of industry. He contends that education was used to tie Black students to a version of Christianity that supported White interests. He references Carter G. Woodson, who declared that this type of education amounted to "Religion Without Letters," designed to ensure that Blacks were "better slaves [with] no reading and writing, no real intelligence." In this respect, Du Bois's critique of Black education was an early example of critical race theory's interest convergence tenet.

Clearly Du Bois knew that the proper education of Black people could cause them to become involved in the political life of the country. DuBois's critiques are valuable in a time where the education of Black people is connected to how well they can be trained for work. Education has become weaponized against Black people to ensure they do not become conscious or spiritually awakened to the power structures that contribute to their oppression.

## Chapter 4

Chapter 4 presents Carter G. Woodson's "The Seat of the Trouble," the first chapter of his hugely important book, *The Mis-Education of the Negro* (Woodson, 1933). Often overlooked in the educational discourse Woodson offers what is one of the most critical perspectives on the education of Black people. In his critique of schools, he discloses how the curriculum contributes to Blacks seeing themselves as inferior beings, causing him to say that schooling for Black people is the worst sort of lynching because "it kills one's aspirations and dooms him to vagabondage and crime." He dissects what is taught in various areas of study, surmising that in each of these areas the subject is taught in a way that benefits those in the dominant group.

He notes that a Black person who has completed his education must always remember above all things to be a "good Negro." All of these problems stem from the fact that Black education is controlled by those outside their race. Although educational policies like *No Child Left Behind*, *Race to the Top*, and *Every Student Succeeds* claim to prioritize education for all, Black students continue to experience schooling that subtly implies they are an inferior people. The inequitable policies and practices such as tracking Black students into general education courses while their White peers take Advanced Placement courses is but one example. Because of these trends, Woodson's critique of curricula and teaching continue to ring true in the twenty-first century.

## Chapter 5

Chapter 5 features Marcus Garvey's essay "Intelligence, Education, Universal Knowledge and How to Get It," which passionately advocates for the acquisition of knowledge. He recommends that Black people should read something of value every day for at least four hours per day. For Garvey history and language were important areas of study. History was important because it captured the experiences and wisdom of those who lived through earlier times; he wrote, "you must fall back on the intelligence of others who came before you and left their records behind." History becomes a tool to guide one in understanding how the present has been impacted by the past.

Using a critical framework, he wrote that the educational system hides the accomplishments of Black people, and he critiqued the White images and narratives that dominated American life, such as the common but mistaken idea that Jesus was White. Garvey advocated strongly for an education that empowered Blacks and prepared them for leadership and spiritual freedom.

## Chapter 6

Chapter 6 presents a fascinating early writing by Martin Luther King Jr., an essay he wrote as a student at Morehouse College called "The Purpose of Education." In this essay, a young King challenged the status quo conception of education as a course of study designed to bring wealth to the student or laborers to the business owners. King argues instead that the purpose of education is to build character and morals. He points out that the true purpose of education is not to develop intelligence alone, as "the most dangerous criminal may be the man gifted with reason, but with no morals." Instead intelligence must be developed in conjunction with character. And above all students must learn to question, to think critically, to sort through the half-lies and propaganda rampant in our world.

Schooling in its current practice has become a place where character and morals have taken a backseat to high-stakes testing and scripted curricula; Dr. King's brief essay is a reminder that learning to navigate and assess the ideologies of racism and egotism is the most important building block of education.

## Chapter 7

In chapter 7, James Baldwin's "A Talk to Teachers" argues that education is organized to perpetuate the aims of society at large and that those in power have the ability to shape education to serve their own interests. Baldwin believes education should be designed to help people to develop critical thinking skills to make decisions in *their* best interest. While society wants to use education to develop citizenry who "simply obey the rules of society" (which Chomsky [2000] called "mis-education") Baldwin is clear that such an approach to education—one that silences people's ability to think critically—is self-destructive, not only for Black people but for all of society. He argues that "the American educational system runs the risk of becoming schizophrenic" if it claims to guarantee rights for all while denying the contributions and humanity of Black people.

An education system in which Black children learn nothing of their actual history serves White oppression, not Black needs: "The reason is that this animal once he suspects his own worth, once he starts believing that he is a man, has begun to attack the entire power structure." He suggests that a true history of the Black man is excluded from education because it would disrupt the entire foundation on which White supremacy is built.

Baldwin believes that the entire curriculum must be changed to offer a multicultural perspective, which would not only liberate Black children but also White children, whose talents and character are currently distorted by the myths that support White supremacy. Most important, Baldwin gives an utterly clear defense of critical pedagogy when he writes that if he were a teacher he would teach Black children that much of which surrounds them is intentionally designed to keep them in a second-class status: "I would try to make each child know that these things are the result of a conspiracy to destroy him." Likewise he finds popular culture with its negative stereotypes of Black people to be "based on fantasies created by very ill people." These perspectives are the very heart of critical pedagogy.

## Chapter 8

Chapter 8 is an abbreviated version of Malcolm X's speech "History Is a Weapon." The speech critiques what is taught during Black History Month. Drawing from historical truths Malcolm X points out that Black history has been limited to the achievements of Black people in the context of how it benefits White people. Providing an analogy, he says, "Just like a dog who runs out in the woods and grabs a rabbit. No matter how hungry the dog is, does he eat it? No, he takes it and lays it at the boss's feet. . . . Every contribution we make, we don't make it for our people, we make it for the man, we make it for the master." He argues that history can be used to liberate or oppress people.

Speaking to the value of Black people gaining a true knowledge of themselves he argues that just as a tree without roots is dead, so is a people who do not have knowledge of their history. He provides an alternative perspective to the dominant narratives that depicted Black people as inferior. Critiquing the term *Negro* through history and etymology he deconstructs it, arguing "that we are not Negroes, and have never been, until we were brought here and made into that. We were scientifically produced by the white man." He documents that Black history goes far beyond the cotton fields of the South and can be found in the origin of the universe. Malcolm's essay is an articulation of what he learned from Elijah Muhammad and can be found in *Message to the Black Man in America.*

**Chapter 9**

Chapter 9 is "Get Knowledge to Benefit Self," a critical analysis by Elijah Muhammad of the keys to Black education. He begins by pointing out that Black people in America need the knowledge of self and of their race's cosmic origin. Muhammad believed that Black children have lost their sense of identity through their continued immersion in a racist environment that makes them feel inferior. To avoid this, he believed Black children should be separated from the influence of White education and placed in their own schools until the age of sixteen. Moreover, they should get an education that will be beneficial to other Blacks—one that makes them independent and able to produce jobs for themselves. He understood historically how Black education was tied to the interest of the ruling class who were the owners of industry. This chapter is seeded with critiques and solutions to the crisis in Black education. Perhaps the most powerful takeaway from the chapter is Elijah Muhammad's definition of knowledge where he states one of the attributes of "Allah" is knowledge.

## CONCLUSION

Educational scholars have asked why critical pedagogy hasn't gained traction in making wholesale changes to the educational landscape. In part, critical pedagogy is still new to the people who have been most underserved and bear the brunt of educational inequality. The paternalism in the field of education has limited powerful Black voices from being heard and as a result limited the changes that educators for social justice claim they would like to see. Many of these educational scholars are dumbfounded when challenged by truths that go beyond their critique of the educational crisis.

This has been a major factor in the lack of progress in education. To speak like James Baldwin and declare that the entire educational system is designed to destroy Black people would be heretical. Multicultural education is accepted as long as it is limited to discrete additions to the curriculum. But critical pedagogy requires a more significant transformation, addressing the structures of power, the skills needed to advocate for true democracy, the materialistic and instrumental goals of Eurocentric education, and the spiritual aspect of movements to eradicate inequities. It addresses what knowledge is taught and what knowledge is excluded, like the efforts of the Million Man March and other powerful movements that are transforming the Black world.

With the insight of the writers featured in this volume, educators and students in the twenty-first century can learn why critical Black educators believed that the education profession was a calling for racial upliftment. It was critical Black pedagogues who shook up the world through their radical critiques and actions to educate their own. These critiques and new educational models go far beyond the academy and include even hip-hop artists like the late Nipsey Hussle who are reaching out in creative ways to impact their local communities. The voices of critical Black pedagogues should be studied if we are truly vested in giving birth to a new and better world.

## REFERENCES

American Education Research Association (AERA). (n.d.). Previous Annual Meetings. https://www.aera.net/Events-Meetings/Annual-Meeting/Previous-Annual-Meetings. Accessed March 7, 2019.

Akbar, N. (1998). *Know thyself.* Tallahassee, FL: Mind Productions and Associates.

———. (2009). The context of African American educational performance. In A. Pitre, R. Ray, E. Pitre, & T. Pitre (Eds.), *Educating African American students: Foundations, curriculum, and experiences* (pp. 19–33). Lanham, MD: Rowman & Littlefield.

Allen, R. (2006). The race problem in the critical pedagogy community. In C. Rossatto, R. Allen, & M. Pruyn (Eds.), *Reinventing critical pedagogy: Widening the circle of anti-oppression education* (pp. 3–20). Lanham, MD: Rowman & Littlefield.

Anderson, James D. (2005). *Foreword.* In W. Watkins (Ed.), *Black protest thought and education* (pp. vi–xiii). New York: Peter Lang.

Apple, M. (1993). The politics of official knowledge: Does a national curriculum make sense? *Teachers College Record, 95*(2): 222–241.

———. (2019). *Ideology and curriculum* (4th ed.). New York: Routledge.

Asante, M. K. (1991). The Afrocentric idea in education. *The Journal of Negro Education, 6*(2): 170–180.

Au, W. (2012). *Critical curriculum studies: Education, consciousness, and the politics of knowing.* New York: Routledge.

Banks, J. (1992). African American scholarship and the evolution of multicultural education. *Journal of Negro Education, 61*(3): 273–286.

Bell, D. (1992). *Faces at the bottom of the well: The permanence of racism.* New York: Basic Books.

Berg, H. (2009). *Elijah Muhammad and Islam.* New York: New York University Press.

Bonilla-Silva, E. (2006). *Racism without racists: Color-blind racism and the persistence of inequality in the United States.* Lanham, MD: Rowman & Littlefield.

Chomsky, N. (2000). *Chomsky on mis-education.* Lanham, MD: Rowman & Littlefield.

Clegg, C. (2014). *An original man: The life and times of Elijah Muhammad.* Chapel Hill, NC: University of North Carolina Press.

Cochrane, M. (2017). University Council for Educational Administration General Convention 2017 Call for Proposals. OrgSync, January 10.

Darder, A., Torres, R. D., & Baltodano, M. P. (2017). *The critical pedagogy reader* (3rd ed.). New York: Routledge.

Essein-Udom, E. U. (1962). *Black nationalism: The search for identity.* Chicago: University of Chicago Press.

Freire, P. (1968/2001). *Pedagogy of the oppressed.* New York: Continuum.

Giroux, H. A. (1985/2001). *Theory and resistance in education: Towards a pedagogy for the opposition* (2nd ed.) (Critical Studies in Education and Culture Series). Santa Barbara, CA: Praeger.

Ladson-Billings, G., & Tate, W. (1995). Toward a critical race theory in education. *Teachers College Record, 97*(1): 47–68.

Lincoln, E. (1994). *Black Muslims in America* (3rd ed.). Chapel Hill, NC: Duke University Press.

Marshall, C., & Oliva, M. (Eds.). (2010). *Leadership for social justice: Making revolutions in education* (2nd ed.). Boston: Pearson.

McLaren, P. (2015). *Life in schools: An introduction to critical pedagogy* (6th ed.). New York: Routledge.

Muhammad, E. (1965). *Message to the Black man in America.* Chicago: Final Call.

Muhammad, J. (2009). *This is the one: We need not look for another.* Chicago: Final Call.

Nieto, S., & Bode, P. (2018). *Affirming diversity: The sociopolitical context of education* (7th ed.). New Jersey: Pearson.

Orelus, P., & Brock, R. (Eds.). (2015). *Interrogating critical pedagogy: Voices of educators of color in the movement.* New York: Routledge.

Pitre, A. (2008). *The struggle for Black history: Foundations for a critical Black pedagogy in education.* Lanham, MD: University Press of America.

———. (2010). *An introduction to Elijah Muhammad studies: The new educational paradigm.* Lanham, MD: University Press of America.

———. (2011). *Freedom fighters: The struggle for Black history in K–12 education.* San Diego: Cognella.

———. (2015). *The educational philosophy of Elijah Muhammad: Education for a new world* (3rd ed.). Lanham, MD: University Press of America.

———. (2017). *Educational leadership and Louis Farrakhan* (Critical Black Pedagogy in Education). Lanham, MD: Rowman & Littlefield.

———. (2018). *Farrakhan and education (2nd edition).* San Diego: Cognella.

Rabaka, R. (2008). *Du Bois's dialectics: Black radical politics and the reconstruction of critical social theory.* Lanham, MD: Lexington Books.

Spring, J. (2011). *The politics of American education.* New York: Routledge.

———. (2016). *Deculturalization and the struggle for equality: A brief history of the education of dominated cultures in United States* (8th ed.). New York: Routledge.

Watkins, W. H. (Ed.). (2005). *Black protest thought and education.* New York: Peter Lang.

Williams, J. (2016). *A portraiture of Black homeschooling in Texas: A descriptive case study.* Unpublished doctoral dissertation. Prairie View, TX: Prairie View A&M University.

Woodson, C. G. (1933/2013). *The mis-education of the Negro.* New York: Tribeca Books.

*Chapter One*

# What to the Slave Is the Fourth of July?

## *1852*

## Frederick Douglass

Mr. President, Friends and Fellow Citizens:

He who could address this audience without a quailing sensation, has stronger nerves than I have. I do not remember ever to have appeared as a speaker before any assembly more shrinkingly, nor with greater distrust of my ability, than I do this day. A feeling has crept over me, quite unfavorable to the exercise of my limited powers of speech. The task before me is one which requires much previous thought and study for its proper performance. I know that apologies of this sort are generally considered flat and unmeaning. I trust, however, that mine will not be so considered. Should I seem at ease, my appearance would much misrepresent me. The little experience I have had in addressing public meetings, in country schoolhouses, avails me nothing on the present occasion.

The papers and placards say, that I am to deliver a 4th [of] July oration. This certainly sounds large, and out of the common way, for it is true that I have often had the privilege to speak in this beautiful Hall, and to address many who now honor me with their presence. But neither their familiar faces, nor the perfect gage I think I have of Corinthian Hall, seems to free me from embarrassment.

The fact is, ladies and gentlemen, the distance between this platform and the slave plantation, from which I escaped, is considerable—and the difficulties to be overcome in getting from the latter to the former, are by no means slight. That I am here today is, to me, a matter of astonishment as well as of gratitude. You will not, therefore, be surprised, if in what I have to say I evince no elaborate preparation, nor grace my speech with any high sounding exordium. With little experience and with less learning, I have been able to throw my thoughts hastily and imperfectly together; and trusting to your patient and generous indulgence, I will proceed to lay them before you.

This, for the purpose of this celebration, is the 4th of July. It is the birthday of your National Independence, and of your political freedom. This, to you, is what the Passover was to the emancipated people of God. It carries your minds back to the day, and to the act of your great deliverance; and to the signs, and to the wonders, associated with that act, and that day. This celebration also marks the beginning of another year of your national life; and reminds you that the Republic of America is now 76 years old. I am glad, fellow-citizens, that your nation is so young. Seventy-six years, though a good old age for a man, is but a mere speck in the life of a nation. Three score years and ten is the allotted time for individual men; but nations number their years by thousands. According to this fact, you are, even now, only in the beginning of your national career, still lingering in the period of childhood. I repeat, I am glad this is so. There is hope in the thought, and hope is much needed, under the dark clouds which lower above the horizon. The eye of the reformer is met with angry flashes, portending disastrous times; but his heart may well beat lighter at the thought that America is young, and that she is still in the impressible stage of her existence. May he not hope that high lessons of wisdom, of justice and of truth, will yet give direction to her destiny? Were the nation older, the patriot's heart might be sadder, and the reformer's brow heavier. Its future might be shrouded in gloom, and the hope of its prophets go out in sorrow. There is consolation in the thought that America is young. Great streams are not easily turned from channels, worn deep in the course of ages. They may sometimes rise in quiet and stately majesty, and inundate the land, refreshing and fertilizing the earth with their mysterious properties. They may also rise in wrath and fury, and bear away, on their angry waves, the accumulated wealth of years of toil and hardship. They, however, gradually flow back to the same old channel, and flow on as serenely as ever. But, while the river may not be turned aside, it may dry up, and leave nothing behind but the withered branch, and the unsightly rock, to howl in the abyss-sweeping wind, the sad tale of departed glory. As with rivers so with nations.

Fellow-citizens, I shall not presume to dwell at length on the associations that cluster about this day. The simple story of it is that, 76 years ago, the people of this country were British subjects. The style and title of your "sovereign people" (in which you now glory) was not then born. You were under the British Crown. Your fathers esteemed the English Government as the home government; and England as the fatherland. This home government, you know, although a considerable distance from your home, did, in the exercise of its parental prerogatives, impose upon its colonial children, such restraints, burdens and limitations, as, in its mature judgment, it deemed wise, right and proper.

But, your fathers, who had not adopted the fashionable idea of this day, of the infallibility of government, and the absolute character of its acts, presumed to differ from the home government in respect to the wisdom and the justice of some of those burdens and restraints. They went so far in their excitement as to pronounce the measures of government unjust, unreasonable, and oppressive, and altogether such as ought not to be quietly submitted to. I scarcely need say, fellow-citizens, that my opinion of those measures fully accords with that of your fathers. Such a declaration of agreement on my part would not be worth much to anybody. It would, certainly, prove nothing, as to what part I might have taken, had I lived during the great controversy of 1776. To say now that America was right, and England wrong, is exceedingly easy. Everybody can say it; the dastard, not less than the noble brave, can flippantly discant on the tyranny of England towards the American Colonies. It is fashionable to do so; but there was a time when to pronounce against England, and in favor of the cause of the colonies, tried men's souls. They who did so were accounted in their day, plotters of mischief, agitators and rebels, dangerous men. To side with the right, against the wrong, with the weak against the strong, and with the oppressed against the oppressor! here lies the merit, and the one which, of all others, seems unfashionable in our day. The cause of liberty may be stabbed by the men who glory in the deeds of your fathers. But, to proceed.

Feeling themselves harshly and unjustly treated by the home government, your fathers, like men of honesty, and men of spirit, earnestly sought redress. They petitioned and remonstrated; they did so in a decorous, respectful, and loyal manner. Their conduct was wholly unexceptionable. This, however, did not answer the purpose. They saw themselves treated with sovereign indifference, coldness and scorn. Yet they persevered. They were not the men to look back.

As the sheet anchor takes a firmer hold, when the ship is tossed by the storm, so did the cause of your fathers grow stronger, as it breasted the chilling blasts of kingly displeasure. The greatest and best of British statesmen admitted its justice, and the loftiest eloquence of the British Senate came to its support. But, with that blindness which seems to be the unvarying characteristic of tyrants, since Pharaoh and his hosts were drowned in the Red Sea, the British Government persisted in the exactions complained of.

The madness of this course, we believe, is admitted now, even by England; but we fear the lesson is wholly lost on our present ruler.

Oppression makes a wise man mad. Your fathers were wise men, and if they did not go mad, they became restive under this treatment. They felt themselves the victims of grievous wrongs, wholly incurable in their colonial capacity. With brave men there is always a remedy for oppression. Just here, the idea of a total separation of the colonies from the crown was born! It was a startling idea, much more so, than we, at this distance of time, regard it.

The timid and the prudent (as has been intimated) of that day, were, of course, shocked and alarmed by it.

Such people lived then, had lived before, and will, probably, ever have a place on this planet; and their course, in respect to any great change, (no matter how great the good to be attained, or the wrong to be redressed by it), may be calculated with as much precision as can be the course of the stars. They hate all changes, but silver, gold and copper change! Of this sort of change they are always strongly in favor.

These people were called Tories in the days of your fathers; and the appellation, probably, conveyed the same idea that is meant by a more modern, though a somewhat less euphonious term, which we often find in our papers, applied to some of our old politicians.

Their opposition to the then dangerous thought was earnest and powerful; but, amid all their terror and affrighted vociferations against it, the alarming and revolutionary idea moved on, and the country with it.

On the 2nd of July, 1776, the old Continental Congress, to the dismay of the lovers of ease, and the worshipers of property, clothed that dreadful idea with all the authority of national sanction. They did so in the form of a resolution; and as we seldom hit upon resolutions, drawn up in our day whose transparency is at all equal to this, it may refresh your minds and help my story if I read it. "Resolved, That these united colonies are, and of right, ought to be free and Independent States; that they are absolved from all allegiance to the British Crown; and that all political connection between them and the State of Great Britain is, and ought to be, dissolved."

Citizens, your fathers made good that resolution. They succeeded; and today you reap the fruits of their success. The freedom gained is yours; and you, therefore, may properly celebrate this anniversary. The 4th of July is the first great fact in your nation's history—the very ring-bolt in the chain of your yet undeveloped destiny.

Pride and patriotism, not less than gratitude, prompt you to celebrate and to hold it in perpetual remembrance. I have said that the Declaration of Independence is the ring-bolt to the chain of your nation's destiny; so, indeed, I regard it. The principles contained in that instrument are saving principles. Stand by those principles, be true to them on all occasions, in all places, against all foes, and at whatever cost.

From the round top of your ship of state, dark and threatening clouds may be seen. Heavy billows, like mountains in the distance, disclose to the leeward huge forms of flinty rocks! That bolt drawn, that chain broken, and all is lost. Cling to this day—cling to it, and to its principles, with the grasp of a storm-tossed mariner to a spar at midnight.

The coming into being of a nation, in any circumstances, is an interesting event. But, besides general considerations, there were peculiar circumstances which make the advent of this republic an event of special attractiveness.

The whole scene, as I look back to it, was simple, dignified and sublime.

The population of the country, at the time, stood at the insignificant number of three millions. The country was poor in the munitions of war. The population was weak and scattered, and the country a wilderness unsubdued. There were then no means of concert and combination, such as exist now. Neither steam nor lightning had then been reduced to order and discipline. From the Potomac to the Delaware was a journey of many days. Under these, and innumerable other disadvantages, your fathers declared for liberty and independence and triumphed.

Fellow Citizens, I am not wanting in respect for the fathers of this republic. The signers of the Declaration of Independence were brave men. They were great men too—great enough to give fame to a great age. It does not often happen to a nation to raise, at one time, such a number of truly great men. The point from which I am compelled to view them is not, certainly, the most favorable; and yet I cannot contemplate their great deeds with less than admiration. They were statesmen, patriots and heroes, and for the good they did, and the principles they contended for, I will unite with you to honor their memory.

They loved their country better than their own private interests; and, though this is not the highest form of human excellence, all will concede that it is a rare virtue, and that when it is exhibited, it ought to command respect. He who will, intelligently, lay down his life for his country, is a man whom it is not in human nature to despise. Your fathers staked their lives, their fortunes, and their sacred honor, on the cause of their country. In their admiration of liberty, they lost sight of all other interests.

They were peace men; but they preferred revolution to peaceful submission to bondage. They were quiet men; but they did not shrink from agitating against oppression. They showed forbearance; but that they knew its limits. They believed in order; but not in the order of tyranny. With them, nothing was "settled" that was not right. With them, justice, liberty and humanity were "final;" not slavery and oppression. You may well cherish the memory of such men. They were great in their day and generation. Their solid manhood stands out the more as we contrast it with these degenerate times.

How circumspect, exact and proportionate were all their movements! How unlike the politicians of an hour! Their statesmanship looked beyond the passing moment, and stretched away in strength into the distant future. They seized upon eternal principles, and set a glorious example in their defense. Mark them!

Fully appreciating the hardship to be encountered, firmly believing in the right of their cause, honorably inviting the scrutiny of an on-looking world, reverently appealing to heaven to attest their sincerity, soundly comprehending the solemn responsibility they were about to assume, wisely measuring the terrible odds against them, your fathers, the fathers of this republic, did, most deliberately, under the inspiration of a glorious patriotism, and with a sublime faith in the great principles of justice and freedom, lay deep the corner-stone of the national superstructure, which has risen and still rises in grandeur around you.

Of this fundamental work, this day is the anniversary. Our eyes are met with demonstrations of joyous enthusiasm. Banners and pennants wave ex-ultingly on the breeze. The din of business, too, is hushed. Even Mammon seems to have quitted his grasp on this day. The ear-piercing fife and the stirring drum unite their accents with the ascending peal of a thousand church bells. Prayers are made, hymns are sung, and sermons are preached in honor of this day; while the quick martial tramp of a great and multitudinous nation, echoed back by all the hills, valleys and mountains of a vast continent, bespeak the occasion one of thrilling and universal interest—a nation's jubilee.

Friends and citizens, I need not enter further into the causes which led to this anniversary. Many of you understand them better than I do. You could instruct me in regard to them. That is a branch of knowledge in which you feel, perhaps, a much deeper interest than your speaker. The causes which led to the separation of the colonies from the British crown have never lacked for a tongue. They have all been taught in your common schools, narrated at your firesides, unfolded from your pulpits, and thundered from your legislative halls, and are as familiar to you as household words. They form the staple of your national poetry and eloquence.

I remember, also, that, as a people, Americans are remarkably familiar with all facts which make in their own favor. This is esteemed by some as a national trait—perhaps a national weakness. It is a fact, that whatever makes for the wealth or for the reputation of Americans, and can be had cheap! will be found by Americans. I shall not be charged with slandering Americans, if I say I think the American side of any question may be safely left in American hands.

I leave, therefore, the great deeds of your fathers to other gentlemen whose claim to have been regularly descended will be less likely to be disputed than mine!

My business, if I have any here today, is with the present. The accepted time with God and his cause is the ever-living now.

> *Trust no future, however pleasant,*
> *Let the dead past bury its dead;*
> *Act, act in the living present,*
> *Heart within, and God overhead.*

We have to do with the past only as we can make it useful to the present and to the future. To all inspiring motives, to noble deeds which can be gained from the past, we are welcome. But now is the time, the important time. Your fathers have lived, died, and have done their work, and have done much of it well. You live and must die, and you must do your work. You have no right to enjoy a child's share in the labor of your fathers, unless your children are to be blest by your labors. You have no right to wear out and waste the hard-earned fame of your fathers to cover your indolence. Sydney Smith tells us that men seldom eulogize the wisdom and virtues of their fathers, but to excuse some folly or wickedness of their own. This truth is not a doubtful one. There are illustrations of it near and remote, ancient and modern. It was fashionable, hundreds of years ago, for the children of Jacob to boast, we have "Abraham to our father," when they had long lost Abraham's faith and spirit. That people contented themselves under the shadow of Abraham's great name, while they repudiated the deeds which made his name great. Need I remind you that a similar thing is being done all over this country today? Need I tell you that the Jews are not the only people who built the tombs of the prophets, and garnished the sepulchres of the righteous? Washington could not die till he had broken the chains of his slaves. Yet his monument is built up by the price of human blood, and the traders in the bodies and souls of men shout—"We have Washington to *our father.*"—Alas! that it should be so; yet so it is.

*The evil that men do, lives after them, The good is oft-interred with their bones.*

Fellow-citizens, pardon me, allow me to ask, why am I called upon to speak here today? What have I, or those I represent, to do with your national independence? Are the great principles of political freedom and of natural justice, embodied in that Declaration of Independence, extended to us? and am I, therefore, called upon to bring our humble offering to the national altar, and to confess the benefits and express devout gratitude for the blessings resulting from your independence to us?

Would to God, both for your sakes and ours, that an affirmative answer could be truthfully returned to these questions! Then would my task be light, and my burden easy and delightful. For who is there so cold, that a nation's sympathy could not warm him? Who so obdurate and dead to the claims of gratitude, that would not thankfully acknowledge such priceless benefits? Who so stolid and selfish, that would not give his voice to swell the hallelujahs of a nation's jubilee, when the chains of servitude had been torn from his limbs? I am not that man. In a case like that, the dumb might eloquently speak, and the "lame man leap as an hart."

But, such is not the state of the case. I say it with a sad sense of the disparity between us. I am not included within the pale of this glorious anniversary! Your high independence only reveals the immeasurable distance between us. The blessings in which you, this day, rejoice, are not enjoyed in common.—The rich inheritance of justice, liberty, prosperity and independence, bequeathed by your fathers, is shared by you, not by me. The sunlight that brought life and healing to you, has brought stripes and death to me. This Fourth [of] July is *yours*, not *mine*. *You* may rejoice, *I* must mourn. To drag a man in fetters into the grand illuminated temple of liberty, and call upon him to join you in joyous anthems, were inhuman mockery and sacrilegious irony. Do you mean, citizens, to mock me, by asking me to speak today? If so, there is a parallel to your conduct. And let me warn you that it is dangerous to copy the example of a nation whose crimes, lowering up to heaven, were thrown down by the breath of the Almighty, burying that nation in irrecoverable ruin! I can today take up the plaintive lament of a peeled and woe-smitten people!

"By the rivers of Babylon, there we sat down. Yea! we wept when we remembered Zion. We hanged our harps upon the willows in the midst thereof. For there, they that carried us away captive, required of us a song; and they who wasted us required of us mirth, saying, Sing us one of the songs of Zion. How can we sing the Lord's song in a strange land? If I forget thee, O Jerusalem, let my right hand forget her cunning. If I do not remember thee, let my tongue cleave to the roof of my mouth."

Fellow-citizens; above your national, tumultuous joy, I hear the mournful wail of millions! whose chains, heavy and grievous yesterday, are, today, rendered more intolerable by the jubilee shouts that reach them. If I do forget, if I do not faithfully remember those bleeding children of sorrow this day, "may my right hand forget her cunning, and may my tongue cleave to the roof of my mouth!" To forget them, to pass lightly over their wrongs, and to chime in with the popular theme, would be treason most scandalous and shocking, and would make me a reproach before God and the world. My subject, then fellow-citizens, is AMERICAN SLAVERY. I shall see, this day, and its popular characteristics, from the slave's point of view. Standing, there, identified with the American bondman, making his wrongs mine, I do not hesitate to declare, with all my soul, that the character and conduct of this nation never looked blacker to me than on this 4th of July! Whether we turn to the declarations of the past, or to the professions of the present, the conduct of the nation seems equally hideous and revolting. America is false to the past, false to the present, and solemnly binds herself to be false to the future. Standing with God and the crushed and bleeding slave on this occasion, I will, in the name of humanity which is outraged, in the name of liberty which is fettered, in the name of the constitution and the Bible, which are disregarded and trampled upon, dare to call in question and to denounce, with all the emphasis I can command, everything that serves to perpetuate slavery—the great sin and shame of America! "I will not equivocate; I will not excuse;" I will use the severest language I can command; and yet not one word shall escape me that any man, whose judgment is not blinded by prejudice, or who is not at heart a slaveholder, shall not confess to be right and just.

But I fancy I hear some one of my audience say, it is just in this circumstance that you and your brother abolitionists fail to make a favorable impression on the public mind. Would you argue more, and denounce less, would you persuade more, and rebuke less, your cause would be much more likely to succeed. But, I submit, where all is plain there is nothing to be argued. What point in the anti-slavery creed would you have me argue? On what branch of the subject do the people of this country need light? Must I undertake to prove that the slave is a man? That point is conceded already. Nobody doubts it. The slaveholders themselves acknowledge it in the enactment of laws for their government. They acknowledge it when they punish disobedience on the part of the slave. There are seventy-two crimes in the State of Virginia, which, if committed by a black man, (no matter how ignorant he be), subject him to the punishment of death; while only two of the same crimes will subject a white man to the like punishment. What is this but the acknowledgement that the slave is a moral, intellectual and responsible being? The manhood of the slave is conceded. It is admitted in the fact that Southern statute books are covered with enactments forbidding, under severe fines and penalties, the teaching of the slave to read or to write. When you can point to any such laws, in reference to the beasts of the field, then I may consent to argue the manhood of the slave. When the dogs in your streets, when the fowls of the air, when the cattle on your hills, when the fish of the sea, and the reptiles that crawl, shall be unable to distinguish the slave from a brute, *then* will I argue with you that the slave is a man!

For the present, it is enough to affirm the equal manhood of the Negro race. Is it not astonishing that, while we are ploughing, planting and reaping, using all kinds of mechanical tools, erecting houses, constructing bridges, building ships, working in metals of brass, iron, copper, silver and gold; that, while we are reading, writing and cyphering, acting as clerks, merchants and secretaries, having among us lawyers, doctors, ministers, poets, authors, editors, orators and teachers; that, while we are engaged in all manner of enterprises common to other men, digging gold in California, capturing the whale in the Pacific, feeding sheep and cattle on the hill-side, living, moving, acting, thinking, planning, living in families as husbands, wives and children, and, above all, confessing and worshipping the Christian's God, and looking hopefully for life and immortality beyond the grave, we are called upon to prove that we are men!

Would you have me argue that man is entitled to liberty? that he is the rightful owner of his own body? You have already declared it. Must I argue the wrongfulness of slavery? Is that a question for Republicans? Is it to be settled by the rules of logic and argumentation, as a matter beset with great difficulty, involving a doubtful application of the principle of justice, hard to be understood? How should I look today, in the presence of Americans, dividing, and subdividing a discourse, to show that men have a natural right

to freedom speaking of it relatively, and positively, negatively, and affirma-
tively. To do so, would be to make myself ridiculous, and to offer an insult to
your understanding.—There is not a man beneath the canopy of heaven, that
does not know that slavery is wrong *for him.*

What, am I to argue that it is wrong to make men brutes, to rob them of
their liberty, to work them without wages, to keep them ignorant of their
relations to their fellow men, to beat them with sticks, to flay their flesh with
the lash, to load their limbs with irons, to hunt them with dogs, to sell them at
auction, to sunder their families, to knock out their teeth, to burn their flesh,
to starve them into obedience and submission to their masters? Must I argue
that a system thus marked with blood, and stained with pollution, is *wrong*?
No! I will not. I have better employments for my time and strength than such
arguments would imply.

What, then, remains to be argued? Is it that slavery is not divine; that God
did not establish it; that our doctors of divinity are mistaken? There is blasphemy in the thought. That which is inhuman, cannot be divine! Who can
reason on such a proposition? They that can, may; I cannot. The time for
such argument is passed.

At a time like this, scorching irony, not convincing argument, is needed.
O! had I the ability, and could I reach the nation's ear, I would, today, pour
out a fiery stream of biting ridicule, blasting reproach, withering sarcasm,
and stern rebuke. For it is not light that is needed, but fire; it is not the gentle
shower, but thunder. We need the storm, the whirlwind, and the earthquake.
The feeling of the nation must be quickened; the conscience of the nation
must be roused; the propriety of the nation must be startled; the hypocrisy of
the nation must be exposed; and its crimes against God and man must be
proclaimed and denounced.

What, to the American slave, is your 4th of July? I answer: a day that
reveals to him, more than all other days in the year, the gross injustice and
cruelty to which he is the constant victim. To him, your celebration is a
sham; your boasted liberty, an unholy license; your national greatness, swell-
ing vanity; your sounds of rejoicing are empty and heartless; your denuncia-
tions of tyrants, brass fronted impudence; your shouts of liberty and equality,
hollow mockery; your prayers and hymns, your sermons and thanksgivings,
with all your religious parade, and solemnity, are, to him, mere bombast,
fraud, deception, impiety, and hypocrisy—a thin veil to cover up crimes
which would disgrace a nation of savages. There is not a nation on the earth
guilty of practices, more shocking and bloody, than are the people of these
United States, at this very hour.

Go where you may, search where you will, roam through all the monar-
chies and despotisms of the old world, travel through South America, search
out every abuse, and when you have found the last, lay your facts by the side

of the everyday practices of this nation, and you will say with me, that, for revolting barbarity and shameless hypocrisy, America reigns without a rival.

Take the American slave-trade, which, we are told by the papers, is especially prosperous just now. Ex-Senator Benton tells us that the price of men was never higher than now. He mentions the fact to show that slavery is in no danger. This trade is one of the peculiarities of American institutions. It is carried on in all the large towns and cities in one-half of this confederacy; and millions are pocketed every year, by dealers in this horrid traffic. In several states, this trade is a chief source of wealth. It is called (in contradistinction to the foreign slave-trade) *"the internal slave trade."* It is, probably, called so, too, in order to divert from it the horror with which the foreign slave-trade is contemplated. That trade has long since been denounced by this government, as piracy. It has been denounced with burning words, from the high places of the nation, as an execrable traffic. To arrest it, to put an end to it, this nation keeps a squadron, at immense cost, on the coast of Africa. Everywhere, in this country, it is safe to speak of this foreign slave-trade, as a most inhuman traffic, opposed alike to the laws of God and of man. The duty to extirpate and destroy it, is admitted even by our DOCTORS OF DIVINITY. In order to put an end to it, some of these last have consented that their colored brethren (nominally free) should leave this country, and establish themselves on the western coast of Africa! It is, however, a notable fact that, while so much execration is poured out by Americans upon those engaged in the foreign slave-trade, the men engaged in the slave-trade between the states pass without condemnation, and their business is deemed honorable.

Behold the practical operation of this internal slave-trade, the American slave-trade, sustained by American politics and America religion. Here you will see men and women reared like swine for the market. You know what is a swine-drover? I will show you a man-drover. They inhabit all our Southern States. They perambulate the country, and crowd the highways of the nation, with droves of human stock. You will see one of these human flesh-jobbers, armed with pistol, whip and bowie-knife, driving a company of a hundred men, women, and children, from the Potomac to the slave market at New Orleans. These wretched people are to be sold singly, or in lots, to suit purchasers. They are food for the cotton-field, and the deadly sugar-mill. Mark the sad procession, as it moves wearily along, and the inhuman wretch who drives them. Hear his savage yells and his blood-chilling oaths, as he hurries on his affrighted captives! There, see the old man, with locks thinned and gray. Cast one glance, if you please, upon that young mother, whose shoulders are bare to the scorching sun, her briny tears falling on the brow of the babe in her arms. See, too, that girl of thirteen, weeping, *yes*! weeping, as she thinks of the mother from whom she has been torn! The drove moves tardily. Heat and sorrow have nearly consumed their strength; suddenly you hear a quick snap, like the discharge of a rifle; the fetters clank, and the chain rattles simultaneously; your ears are saluted with a scream, that seems to have torn its way to the center of your soul! The crack you heard, was the sound of the slave-whip; the scream you heard, was from the woman you saw with the babe. Her speed had faltered under the weight of her child and her chains! that gash on her shoulder tells her to move on. Follow the drove to New Orleans. Attend the auction; see men examined like horses; see the forms of women rudely and brutally exposed to the shocking gaze of American slave-buyers. See this drove sold and separated forever; and never forget the deep, sad sobs that arose from that scattered multitude. Tell me citizens, WHERE, under the sun, you can witness a spectacle more fiendish and shocking. Yet this is but a glance at the American slave-trade, as it exists, at this moment, in the ruling part of the United States.

I was born amid such sights and scenes. To me the American slave-trade is a terrible reality. When a child, my soul was often pierced with a sense of its horrors. I lived on Philpot Street, Fell's Point, Baltimore, and have watched from the wharves, the slave ships in the Basin, anchored from the shore, with their cargoes of human flesh, waiting for favorable winds to waft them down the Chesapeake. There was, at that time, a grand slave mart kept at the head of Pratt Street, by Austin Woldfolk. His agents were sent into every town and county in Maryland, announcing their arrival, through the papers, and on flaming "*hand-bills*," headed CASH FOR NEGROES. These men were generally well dressed men, and very captivating in their manners. Ever ready to drink, to treat, and to gamble. The fate of many a slave has depended upon the turn of a single card; and many a child has been snatched from the arms of its mother by bargains arranged in a state of brutal drunkenness.

The flesh-mongers gather up their victims by dozens, and drive them, chained, to the general depot at Baltimore. When a sufficient number have been collected here, a ship is chartered, for the purpose of conveying the forlorn crew to Mobile, or to New Orleans. From the slave prison to the ship, they are usually driven in the darkness of night; for since the antislavery agitation, a certain caution is observed.

In the deep still darkness of midnight, I have been often aroused by the dead heavy footsteps, and the piteous cries of the chained gangs that passed our door. The anguish of my boyish heart was intense; and I was often consoled, when speaking to my mistress in the morning, to hear her say that the custom was very wicked; that she hated to hear the rattle of the chains, and the heart-rending cries. I was glad to find one who sympathized with me in my horror.

Fellow-citizens, this murderous traffic is, today, in active operation in this boasted republic. In the solitude of my spirit, I see clouds of dust raised on the highways of the South; I see the bleeding footsteps; I hear the doleful wail of fettered humanity, on the way to the slave-markets, where the victims are to be sold like *horses, sheep,* and *swine,* knocked off to the highest bidder. There I see the tenderest ties ruthlessly broken, to gratify the lust, caprice and rapacity of the buyers and sellers of men. My soul sickens at the sight.

> *Is this the land your Fathers loved,*
> *The freedom which they toiled to win?*
> *Is this the earth whereon they moved?*
> *Are these the graves they slumber in?*

But a still more inhuman, disgraceful, and scandalous state of things remains to be presented. By an act of the American Congress, not yet two years old, slavery has been nationalized in its most horrible and revolting form. By that act, Mason and Dixon's line has been obliterated; New York has become as Virginia; and the power to hold, hunt, and sell men, women, and children as slaves remains no longer a mere state institution, but is now an institution of the whole United States. The power is co-extensive with the Star-Spangled Banner and American Christianity. Where these go, may also go the merciless slave-hunter. Where these are, man is not sacred. He is a bird for the sportsman's gun. By that most foul and fiendish of all human decrees, the liberty and person of every man are put in peril. Your broad republican domain is hunting ground for *men.* Not for thieves and robbers, enemies of society, merely, but for men guilty of no crime. Your lawmakers have commanded all good citizens to engage in this hellish sport. Your President, your Secretary of State, our *lords, nobles,* and ecclesiastics, enforce, as a duty you owe to your free and glorious country, and to your God, that you do this accursed thing. Not fewer than forty Americans have, within the past two years, been hunted down and, without a moment's warning, hurried away in chains, and consigned to slavery and excruciating torture. Some of these have had wives and children, dependent on them for bread; but of this, no account was made. The right of the hunter to his prey stands superior to the right of marriage, and to *all* rights in this republic, the rights of God included! For black men there are neither law, justice, humanity, not religion. The Fugitive Slave *Law* makes mercy to them a crime; and bribes the judge who tries them. An American judge gets ten dollars for every victim he consigns to slavery, and five, when he fails to do so. The oath of any two villains is sufficient, under this hell-black enactment, to send the most pious and exemplary black man into the remorseless jaws of slavery! His own testimony is nothing. He can bring no witnesses for himself. The minister of American justice is bound by the law to hear but *one* side; and *that* side, is the side of the oppressor. Let this damning fact be perpetually told. Let it be thundered around the world, that, in tyrant-killing, king-hating, people-loving, democratic, Christian America, the seats of justice are filled with judges, who hold their offices under an open and palpable *bribe*, and are bound, in deciding in the case of a man's liberty, *hear only his accusers*!

In glaring violation of justice, in shameless disregard of the forms of administering law, in cunning arrangement to entrap the defenseless, and in diabolical intent, this Fugitive Slave Law stands alone in the annals of tyrannical legislation. I doubt if there be another nation on the globe, having the brass and the baseness to put such a law on the statute-book. If any man in this assembly thinks differently from me in this matter, and feels able to disprove my statements, I will gladly confront him at any suitable time and place he may select.

I take this law to be one of the grossest infringements of Christian Liberty, and, if the churches and ministers of our country were not stupidly blind, or most wickedly indifferent, they, too, would so regard it.

At the very moment that they are thanking God for the enjoyment of civil and religious liberty, and for the right to worship God according to the dictates of their own consciences, they are utterly silent in respect to a law which robs religion of its chief significance, and makes it utterly worthless to a world lying in wickedness. Did this law concern the *"mint, anise, and cumin"*—abridge the right to sing psalms, to partake of the sacrament, or to engage in any of the ceremonies of religion, it would be smitten by the thunder of a thousand pulpits. A general shout would go up from the church, demanding *repeal, repeal, instant repeal*!—And it would go hard with that politician who presumed to solicit the votes of the people without inscribing this motto on his banner. Further, if this demand were not complied with, another Scotland would be added to the history of religious liberty, and the stern old Covenanters would be thrown into the shade. A John Knox would be seen at every church door, and heard from every pulpit, and Fillmore would have no more quarter than was shown by Knox, to the beautiful, but treacherous queen Mary of Scotland. The fact that the church of our country, (with fractional exceptions), does not esteem "the Fugitive Slave Law" as a declaration of war against religious liberty, implies that that church regards religion simply as a form of worship, an empty ceremony, and *not* a vital principle, requiring active benevolence, justice, love and good will towards man. It esteems sacrifice above mercy; psalm-singing above right doing; solemn meetings above practical righteousness. A worship that can be conducted by persons who refuse to give shelter to the houseless, to give bread to the hungry, clothing to the naked, and who enjoin obedience to a law forbidding these acts of mercy, is a curse, not a blessing to mankind. The Bible addresses all such persons as "scribes, Pharisees, hypocrites, who pay tithe of *mint, anise*, and *cumin*, and have omitted the weightier matters of the law, judgment, mercy and faith."

But the church of this country is not only indifferent to the wrongs of the slave, it actually takes sides with the oppressors. It has made itself the bulwark of American slavery, and the shield of American slave-hunters. Many of its most eloquent Divines. who stand as the very lights of the church, have shamelessly given the sanction of religion and the Bible to the whole slave system. They have taught that man may, properly, be a slave; that the relation of master and slave is ordained of God; that to send back an escaped bond-man to his master is clearly the duty of all the followers of the Lord Jesus Christ; and this horrible blasphemy is palmed off upon the world for Christianity.

For my part, I would say, welcome infidelity! welcome atheism! welcome anything! in preference to the gospel, *as preached by those Divines*! They convert the very name of religion into an engine of tyranny, and barbarous cruelty, and serve to confirm more infidels, in this age, than all the infidel writings of Thomas Paine, Voltaire, and Bolingbroke, put together, have done! These ministers make religion a cold and flinty-hearted thing, having neither principles of right action, nor bowels of compassion. They strip the love of God of its beauty, and leave the throng of religion a huge, horrible, repulsive form. It is a religion for oppressors, tyrants, man-stealers, and *thugs*. It is not that *"pure and undefiled religion"* which is from above, and which is *"first pure, then peaceable, easy to be entreated*, full of mercy and good fruits, *without partiality, and without hypocrisy."* But a religion which favors the rich against the poor; which exalts the proud above the humble; which divides mankind into two classes, tyrants and slaves; which says to the man in chains, *stay there*; and to the oppressor, *oppress on*; it is a religion which may be professed and enjoyed by all the robbers and enslavers of mankind; it makes God a respecter of persons, denies his fatherhood of the race, and tramples in the dust the great truth of the brotherhood of man. All this we affirm to be true of the popular church, and the popular worship of our land and nation—a religion, a church, and a worship which, on the authority of inspired wisdom, we pronounce to be an abomination in the sight of God. In the language of Isaiah, the American church might be well addressed, "Bring no more vain ablations; incense is an abomination unto me: the new moons and Sabbaths, the calling of assemblies, I cannot away with; it is iniquity even the solemn meeting. Your new moons and your appointed feasts my soul hateth. They are a trouble to me; I am weary to bear them; and when ye spread forth your hands I will hide mine eyes from you. Yea! when ye make many prayers, I will not hear. YOUR HANDS ARE FULL OF BLOOD; cease to do evil, learn to do well; seek judgment; relieve the oppressed; judge for the fatherless; plead for the widow."

The American church is guilty, when viewed in connection with what it is doing to uphold slavery; but it is superlatively guilty when viewed in connection with its ability to abolish slavery. The sin of which it is guilty is one of omission as well as of commission. Albert Barnes but uttered what the common sense of every man at all observant of the actual state of the case will receive as truth, when he declared that "There is no power out of the church that could sustain slavery an hour, if it were not sustained in it."

Let the religious press, the pulpit, the Sunday school, the conference meeting, the great ecclesiastical, missionary, Bible and tract associations of the land array their immense powers against slavery and slave-holding; and the whole system of crime and blood would be scattered to the winds; and that they do not do this involves them in the most awful responsibility of which the mind can conceive.

In prosecuting the anti-slavery enterprise, we have been asked to spare the church, to spare the ministry; but *how*, we ask, could such a thing be done? We are met on the threshold of our efforts for the redemption of the slave, by the church and ministry of the country, in battle arrayed against us; and we are compelled to fight or flee. From *what* quarter, I beg to know, has proceeded a fire so deadly upon our ranks, during the last two years, as from the Northern pulpit? As the champions of oppressors, the chosen men of American theology have appeared—men, honored for their so-called piety, and their real learning. The Lords of Buffalo, the Springs of New York, the Lathrops of Auburn, the Coxes and Spencers of Brooklyn, the Gannets and Sharps of Boston, the Deweys of Washington, and other great religious lights of the land have, in utter denial of the authority of *Him* by whom they professed to be called to the ministry, deliberately taught us, against the example of the Hebrews and against the remonstrance of the Apostles, they teach *that we ought to obey man's law before the law of God.*

My spirit wearies of such blasphemy; and how such men can be supported, as the "standing types and representatives of Jesus Christ," is a mystery which I leave others to penetrate. In speaking of the American church, however, let it be distinctly understood that I mean the great mass of the religious organizations of our land. There are exceptions, and I thank God that there are. Noble men may be found, scattered all over these Northern States, of whom Henry Ward Beecher of Brooklyn, Samuel J. May of Syracuse, and my esteemed friend (Rev. R. R. Raymond) on the platform, are shining examples; and let me say further, that upon these men lies the duty to inspire our ranks with high religious faith and zeal, and to cheer us on in the great mission of the slave's redemption from his chains.

One is struck with the difference between the attitude of the American church towards the anti-slavery movement, and that occupied by the churches in England towards a similar movement in that country. There, the church, true to its mission of ameliorating, elevating, and improving the condition of mankind, came forward promptly, bound up the wounds of the West Indian slave, and restored him to his liberty. There, the question of emancipation was a high religious question. It was demanded, in the name of humanity, and according to the law of the living God. The Sharps, the Clarksons, the Wilberforces, the Buxtons, and Burchells and the Knibbs, were alike famous for their piety, and for their philanthropy. The anti-slavery movement *there* was not an anti-church movement, for the reason that the church took its full share in prosecuting that movement: and the anti-slavery movement in this country will cease to be an anti-church movement, when the church of this country shall assume a favorable, instead of a hostile position towards that movement. Americans! your republican politics, not less than your republican religion, are flagrantly inconsistent. You boast of your love of liberty, your superior civilization, and your pure Christianity, while the whole political power of the nation (as embodied in the two great political parties), is solemnly pledged to support and perpetuate the enslavement of three millions of your countrymen. You hurl your anathemas at the crowned headed tyrants of Russia and Austria, and pride yourselves on your Democratic institutions, while you yourselves consent to be the mere *tools* and *body-guards* of the tyrants of Virginia and Carolina. You invite to your shores fugitives of oppression from abroad, honor them with banquets, greet them with ovations, cheer them, toast them, salute them, protect them, and pour out your money to them like water; but the fugitives from your own land you advertise, hunt, arrest, shoot and kill. You glory in your refinement and your universal education yet you maintain a system as barbarous and dreadful as ever stained the character of a nation—a system begun in avarice, supported in pride, and perpetuated in cruelty. You shed tears over fallen Hungary, and make the sad story of her wrongs the theme of your poets, statesmen and orators, till your gallant sons are ready to fly to arms to vindicate her cause against her oppressors; but, in regard to the ten thousand wrongs of the American slave, you would enforce the strictest silence, and would hail him as an enemy of the nation who dares to make those wrongs the subject of public discourse! You are all on fire at the mention of liberty for France or for Ireland; but are as cold as an iceberg at the thought of liberty for the enslaved of America. You discourse eloquently on the dignity of labor; yet, you sustain a system which, in its very essence, casts a stigma upon labor. You can bare your bosom to the storm of British artillery to throw off a threepenny tax on tea; and yet wring the last hard-earned farthing from the grasp of the black laborers of your country. You profess to believe "that, of one blood, God made all nations of men to dwell on the face of all the earth," and hath commanded all men, everywhere to love one another; yet you notoriously hate, (and glory in your hatred), all men whose skins are not colored like your own. You declare, before the world, and are understood by the world to declare, that you "*hold these truths to be self evident, that all men are created equal; and are endowed by their Creator with certain inalienable rights; and that, among these are, life, liberty, and the pursuit of happiness*;" and yet, you hold securely, in a bondage which, according to your own Thomas Jefferson, "*is worse than ages of that which your fathers rose in rebellion to oppose,*" a *seventh part* of the inhabitants of your country.

Fellow-citizens! I will not enlarge further on your national inconsistencies. The existence of slavery in this country brands your republicanism as a sham, your humanity as a base pretence, and your Christianity as a lie. It destroys your moral power abroad; it corrupts your politicians at home. It saps the foundation of religion; it makes your name a hissing, and a bye-word to a mocking earth. It is the antagonistic force in your government, the only thing that seriously disturbs and endangers your *Union*. It fetters your progress; it is the enemy of improvement, the deadly foe of education; it fosters pride; it breeds insolence; it promotes vice; it shelters crime; it is a curse to the earth that supports it; and yet, you cling to it, as if it were the sheet anchor of all your hopes. Oh! be warned! be warned! a horrible reptile is coiled up in your nation's bosom; the venomous creature is nursing at the tender breast of your youthful republic; *for the love of God*, tear away, and fling from you the hideous monster, and *let the weight of twenty millions crush and destroy it forever*!

But it is answered in reply to all this, that precisely what I have now denounced is, in fact, guaranteed and sanctioned by the Constitution of the United States; that the right to hold and to hunt slaves is a part of that Constitution framed by the illustrious Fathers of this Republic.

Then, I dare to affirm, notwithstanding all I have said before, your fathers stooped, basely stooped

> *To palter with us in a double sense:*
> *And keep the word of promise to the ear,*
> *But break it to the heart.*

And instead of being the honest men I have before declared them to be, they were the veriest imposters that ever practiced on mankind. This is the inevitable conclusion, and from it there is no escape. But I differ from those who charge this baseness on the framers of the Constitution of the United States. It is a slander upon their memory, at least, so I believe. There is not time now to argue the constitutional question at length—nor have I the ability to discuss it as it ought to be discussed. The subject has been handled with masterly power by Lysander Spooner, Esq., by William Goodell, by Samuel E. Sewall, Esq., and last, though not least, by Gerritt Smith, Esq. These gentlemen have, as I think, fully and clearly vindicated the Constitution from any design to support slavery for an hour.

Fellow-citizens! there is no matter in respect to which, the people of the North have allowed themselves to be so ruinously imposed upon, as that of the pro-slavery character of the Constitution. In that instrument I hold there is neither warrant, license, nor sanction of the hateful thing; but, interpreted as it ought to be interpreted, the Constitution is a GLORIOUS LIBERTY DOC-

UMENT. Read its preamble, consider its purposes. Is slavery among them? Is it at the gateway? or is it in the temple? It is neither. While I do not intend to argue this question on the present occasion, let me ask, if it be not somewhat singular that, if the Constitution were intended to be, by its framers and adopters, a slave-holding instrument, why neither slavery, slaveholding, nor slave can anywhere be found in it. What would be thought of an instrument, drawn up, legally drawn up, for the purpose of entitling the city of Rochester to a track of land, in which no mention of land was made? Now, there are certain rules of interpretation, for the proper understanding of all legal instruments. These rules are well established. They are plain, common-sense rules, such as you and I, and all of us, can understand and apply, without having passed years in the study of law. I scout the idea that the question of the constitutionality or unconstitutionality of slavery is not a question for the people. I hold that every American citizen has a right to form an opinion of the constitution, and to propagate that opinion, and to use all honorable means to make his opinion the prevailing one. Without this right, the liberty of an American citizen would be as insecure as that of a Frenchman. Ex-Vice-President Dallas tells us that the Constitution is an object to which no American mind can be too attentive, and no American heart too devoted. He further says, the Constitution, in its words, is plain and intelligible, and is meant for the home-bred, unsophisticated understandings of our fellow-citizens. Senator Berrien tell[s] us that the Constitution is the fundamental law, that which controls all others. The charter of our liberties, which every citizen has a personal interest in understanding thoroughly. The testimony of Senator Breese, Lewis Cass, and many others that might be named, who are everywhere esteemed as sound lawyers, so regard the constitution. I take it, therefore, that it is not presumption in a private citizen to form an opinion of that instrument.

Now, take the Constitution according to its plain reading, and I defy the presentation of a single pro-slavery clause in it. On the other hand it will be found to contain principles and purposes, entirely hostile to the existence of slavery.

I have detained my audience entirely too long already. At some future period I will gladly avail myself of an opportunity to give this subject a full and fair discussion.

Allow me to say, in conclusion, notwithstanding the dark picture I have this day presented of the state of the nation, I do not despair of this country. There are forces in operation, which must inevitably work the downfall of slavery. "The arm of the Lord is not shortened," and the doom of slavery is certain. I, therefore, leave off where I began, with hope. While drawing encouragement from the Declaration of Independence, the great principles it contains, and the genius of American Institutions, my spirit is also cheered by the obvious tendencies of the age. Nations do not now stand in the same relation to each other that they did ages ago. No nation can now shut itself up from the surrounding world, and trot round in the same old path of its fathers without interference. The time was when such could be done. Long established customs of hurtful character could formerly fence themselves in, and do their evil work with social impunity. Knowledge was then confined and enjoyed by the privileged few, and the multitude walked on in mental darkness. But a change has now come over the affairs of mankind. Walled cities and empires have become unfashionable. The arm of commerce has borne away the gates of the strong city. Intelligence is penetrating the darkest corners of the globe. It makes its pathway over and under the sea, as well as on the earth. Wind, steam, and lightning are its chartered agents. Oceans no longer divide, but link nations together. From Boston to London is now a holiday excursion. Space is comparatively annihilated. Thoughts expressed on one side of the Atlantic, are distinctly heard on the other. The far off and almost fabulous Pacific rolls in grandeur at our feet. The Celestial Empire, the mystery of ages, is being solved. The fiat of the Almighty, "Let there be Light," has not yet spent its force. No abuse, no outrage whether in taste, sport or avarice, can now hide itself from the all-pervading light. The iron shoe, and crippled foot of China must be seen, in contrast with nature. Africa must rise and put on her yet unwoven garment. "Ethiopia shall stretch out her hand unto God." In the fervent aspirations of William Lloyd Garrison, I say, and let every heart join in saying it:

> *God speed the year of jubilee*
> *The wide world o'er*
> *When from their galling chains set free,*
> *Th' oppress'd shall vilely bend the knee,*
> *And wear the yoke of tyranny*
> *Like brutes no more.*
> *That year will come, and freedom's reign,*
> *To man his plundered fights again*
> *Restore.*
> *God speed the day when human blood*
> *Shall cease to flow!*
> *In every clime be understood,*
> *The claims of human brotherhood,*
> *And each return for evil, good,*
> *Not blow for blow;*
> *That day will come all feuds to end.*
> *And change into a faithful friend*
> *Each foe.*
> *God speed the hour, the glorious hour,*
> *When none on earth*
> *Shall exercise a lordly power,*
> *Nor in a tyrant's presence cower;*
> *But all to manhood's stature tower,*

*By equal birth!*
*That hour will come, to each, to all,*
*And from his prison-house, the thrall*
*Go forth.*
*Until that year, day, hour, arrive,*
*With head, and heart, and hand I'll strive,*
*To break the rod, and rend the gyve,*
*The spoiler of his prey deprive —*
*So witness Heaven!*
*And never from my chosen post,*
*Whate'er the peril or the cost,*
*Be driven.*

## REFLECTIVE ACTIVITIES

1. What are some of the main points in Frederick Douglass's speech that stand out to you?
2. Briefly discuss how this speech demonstrates courageous leadership. Identify a few key points using direct quotes from the speech to support your position.
3. Imagine Douglass speaking to educators in the 21st century in a speech entitled, "What to Black people is the school in the 21st century? Using the same critical approach in his Fourth of July speech, outline a few points that you think he would say regarding the education of Black people in the 21st century.
4. Identify a hip hop artist that has lyrics that align with Douglass's critique of American society. Provide at least four examples of these similarities by comparing the lyrics to points raised in the speech.

*Chapter Two*

# The Awakening of the Negro

## *1896*

## Booker T. Washington

"It is through the dairy farm, the truck garden, the trades, and commercial life, largely, that the negro is to find his way to the enjoyment of all his rights."

Someone may be tempted to ask, has not the negro boy or girl as good a right to study a French grammar and instrumental music as the white youth? I answer, Yes, but in the present condition of the negro race in this country there is need of something more. Perhaps I may be forgiven for the seeming egotism if I mention the expansion of my own life partly as an example of what I mean. My earliest recollection is of a small one-room log hut on a large slave plantation in Virginia. After the close of the war, while working in the coal-mines of West Virginia for the support of my mother, I heard in some accidental way of the Hampton Institute. When I learned that it was an institution where a black boy could study, could have a chance to work for his board, and at the same time be taught how to work and to realize the dignity of labor, I resolved to go there. Bidding my mother good-by, I started out one morning to find my way to Hampton, though I was almost penniless and had no definite idea where Hampton was. By walking, begging rides, and paying for a portion of the journey on the steam-cars, I finally succeeded in reaching the city of Richmond, Virginia. I was without money or friends. I slept under a sidewalk, and by working on a vessel next day I earned money to continue my way to the institute, where I arrived with a surplus of fifty cents. At Hampton I found the opportunity—in the way of buildings, teachers, and industries provided by the generous—to get training in the classroom and by practical touch with industrial life, to learn thrift, economy, and push. I was surrounded by an atmosphere of business, Christian influence, and a spirit of self-help that seemed to have awakened every faculty in me and caused me for the first time to realize what it meant to be a man instead of a piece of property.

A year-by-year catalogue of some of the magazine's most momentous work. While there I resolved that when I had finished the course of training I would go into the far South, into the Black Belt of the South, and give my life to providing the same kind of opportunity for self-reliance and self-awakening that I had found provided for me at Hampton. My work began at Tuskegee, Alabama, in 1881, in a small shanty and church, with one teacher and thirty students, without a dollar's worth of property. The spirit of work and of industrial thrift, with aid from the State and generosity from the North, has enabled us to develop an institution of eight hundred students gathered from nineteen States, with seventy-nine instructors, fourteen hundred acres of land, and thirty buildings, including large and small; in all, property valued at $280,000. Twenty-five industries have been organized, and the whole work is carried on at an annual cost of about $80,000 in cash; two fifths of the annual expense so far has gone into permanent plant.

What is the object of all this outlay? First, it must be borne in mind that we have in the South a peculiar and unprecedented state of things. It is of the utmost importance that our energy be given to meeting conditions that exist right about us rather than conditions that existed centuries ago or that exist in countries a thousand miles away. What are the cardinal needs among the colored people in the South, most of whom are to be found on the plantations? Roughly, these needs may be stated as food, clothing, shelter, education, proper habits, and a settlement of race relations. The seven million of colored people of the South cannot be reached directly by any missionary agency, but they can be reached by sending out among them strong selected young men and women, with the proper training of head, hand, and heart, who will live among these masses and show them how to lift themselves up.

The problem that the Tuskegee Institute keeps before itself constantly is how to prepare these leaders. From the outset, in connection with religious and academic training, it has emphasized industrial or hand training as a means of finding the way out of present conditions. First, we have found the industrial teaching useful in giving the student a chance to work out a portion of his expenses while in school. Second, the school furnishes labor that has an economic value, and at the same time gives the student a chance to acquire knowledge and a skill while performing the labor. Most of all, we find the industrial system valuable in teaching economy, thrift, and the dignity of labor, and in giving moral backbone to students. The fact that a student goes out into the world conscious of his power to build a house or a wagon, or to make a harness, gives him a certain confidence and moral independence that he would not possess without such training.

A more detailed example of our methods at Tuskegee may be of interest. For example, we cultivate by student labor six hundred and fifty acres of land. The object is not only to cultivate the land in a way to make it pay our boarding department, but at the same time to teach the students, in addition to the practical works, something of the chemistry of the soil, the best methods of drainage, dairying, the cultivation of fruit, the care of livestock and tools, and scores of other lessons needed by a people whose main dependence is on agriculture. Notwithstanding that eighty-five per cent of the colored people in the South live by agriculture in some form, aside from what has been done by Hampton, Tuskegee, and one or two other institutions practically nothing has been attempted in the direction of teaching them about the very industry from which the masses of our people must get their subsistence. Friends have recently provided means for the erection of a large new chapel at Tuskegee. Our students have made the bricks for this chapel. A large part of the timber is sawed by students at our own sawmill, the plans are drawn by our teacher of architecture and mechanical drawing, and students do the brick-masonry, plastering, painting, carpentry work, tinning, slatting, and make most of the furniture. Practically, the whole chapel will be built and furnished by student labor; in the end the school will have the building for permanent use, and the students will have a knowledge of the trades employed in its construction. In this way all but three of the thirty buildings on the grounds have been erected. While the young men do the kinds of work I have mentioned, the young women to a large extent make, mend, and launder the clothing of the young men, and thus are taught important industries.

One of the objections sometimes urged against industrial education for the negro is that it aims merely to teach him to work on the same plan that he was made to follow when in slavery. This is far from being the object at Tuskegee. At the head of each of the twenty-five industrial departments we have an intelligent and competent instructor, just as we have in our history classes, so that the student is taught not only practical brick-masonry, for example, but also the underlying principles of that industry, the mathematics and the mechanical and architectural drawing. Or he is taught how to become master of the forces of nature so that, instead of cultivating corn in the old way, he can use a corn cultivator, that lays off the furrows, drops the corn into them, and covers it, and in this way he can do more work than three men by the old process of corn-planting; at the same time much of the toil is eliminated and labor is dignified. In a word, the constant aim is to show the student how to put brains into every process of labor; how to bring his knowledge of mathematics and the sciences into farming, carpentry, forging, foundry work; how to dispense as soon as possible with the old form of ante-bellum labor. In the erection of the chapel just referred to, instead of letting the money which was given us go into outside hands, we make it accomplish three objects: first, it provides the chapel; second, it gives the students a chance to get a practical knowledge of the trades connected with building; and third, it enables them to earn something toward the payment of board while receiving academic and industrial training.

Having been fortified at Tuskegee by education of mind, skill of hand, Christian character, ideas of thrift, economy, and push, and a spirit of independence, the student is sent out to become a centre of influence and light in showing the masses of our people in the Black Belt of the South how to lift themselves up. How can this be done? I give but one or two examples. Ten years ago a young colored man came to the institute from one of the large plantation districts; he studied in the class-room a portion of the time, and received practical and theoretical training on the farm the remainder of the time. Having finished his course at Tuskegee, he returned to his plantation home, which was in a county where the colored people outnumber the whites six to one, as is true of many of the counties in the Black Belt of the South. He found the negroes in debt. Ever since the war they had been mortgaging their crops for the food on which to live while the crops were growing. The majority of them were living from hand to mouth on rented land, in small, one-room log cabins, and attempting to pay a rate of interest on their advances that ranged from fifteen to forty per cent per annum. The school had been taught in a wreck of a log cabin, with no apparatus, and had never been in session longer than three months out of twelve. With as many as eight or ten persons of all ages and conditions and of both sexes huddled together in one cabin year after year, and with a minister whose only aim was to work upon the emotions of the people, one can imagine something of the moral and religious state of the community.

But the remedy. In spite, of the evil the negro got the habit of work from slavery. The rank and file of the race, especially those on the Southern plantations, work hard, but the trouble is, what they earn gets away from them in high rents, crop mortgages, whiskey, snuff, cheap jewelry, and the like. The young man just referred to had been trained at Tuskegee, as most of our graduates are, to meet just this condition of things. He took the three months' public school as a nucleus for his work. Then he organized the older people into a club, or conference, that held meetings every week. In these meetings he taught the people in a plain, simple manner how to save their money, how to farm in a better way, how to sacrifice,—to live on bread and potatoes, if need be, till they could get out of debt, and begin the buying of lands.

Soon a large proportion of the people were in condition to make contracts for the buying of homes (land is very cheap in the South), and to live without mortgaging their crops. Not only this: under the guidance and leadership of this teacher, the first year that he was among them they learned how, by contributions in money and labor, to build a neat, comfortable schoolhouse that replaced the wreck of a log cabin formerly used. The following year the weekly meetings were continued, and two months were added to the original three months of school. The next year two more months were added. The improvement has gone on, until now these people have every year an eight months' school.

I wish my readers could have the chance that I have had of going into this community. I wish they could look into the faces of the people and see them beaming with hope and delight. I wish they could see the two or three room cottages that have taken the place of the usual one-room cabin, the well-cultivated farms, and the religious life of the people that now means something more than the name. The teacher has a good cottage and a well-kept farm that serve as models. In a word, a complete revolution has been wrought in the industrial, educational, and religious life of this whole community by reason of the fact that they have had this leader, this guide and object-lesson, to show them how to take the money and effort that had hitherto been scattered to the wind in mortgages and high rents, in whiskey and gewgaws, and concentrate them in the direction of their own uplifting. One community on its feet presents an object-lesson for the adjoining communities, and soon improvements show themselves in other places.

Another student who received academic and industrial training at Tuskegee established himself, three years ago, as a blacksmith and wheelwright in a community, and, in addition to the influence of his successful business enterprise, he is fast making the same kind of changes in the life of the people about him that I have just recounted. It would be easy for me to fill many pages describing the influence of the Tuskegee graduates in every part of the South. We keep it constantly in the minds of our students and graduates that the industrial or material condition of the masses of our people must be improved, as well as the intellectual, before there can be any permanent change in their moral and religious life. We find it a pretty hard thing to make a good Christian of a hungry man. No matter how much our people "get happy" and "shout" in church, if they go home at night from church hungry, they are tempted to find something before morning. This is a principle of human nature, and is not confined to the negro.

The negro has within him immense power for self-uplifting, but for years it will be necessary to guide and stimulate him. The recognition of this power led us to organize, five years ago, what is now known as the Tuskegee negro Conference,—a gathering that meets every February, and is composed of about eight hundred representative colored men and women from all sections of the Black Belt. They come in ox-carts, mule-carts, buggies, on muleback and horseback, on foot, by railroad; some traveling all night in order to be present. The matters considered at the conferences are those that the colored people have it within their power to control: such as the evils of the mortgage system, the one-room cabin, buying on credit, the importance of owning a home and of putting money in the bank, how to build schoolhouses and prolong the school term, and how to improve their moral and religious condition.

As a single example of the results, one delegate reported that since the conferences were started five years ago eleven people in his neighborhood had bought homes, fourteen had got out of debt, and [a] number had stopped mortgaging their crops. Moreover, a school-house had been built by the people themselves, and the school term had been extended from three to six months; and with a look of triumph he exclaimed, "We is done stopped libin' in de ashes!"

Besides this negro Conference for the masses of the people, we now have a gathering at the same time known as the Workers' Conference, composed of the officers and instructors in the leading colored schools of the South. After listening to the story of the conditions and needs from the people themselves, the Workers' Conference finds much food for thought and discussion.

Nothing else so soon brings about right relations between the two races in the South as the industrial progress of the negro. Friction between the races will pass away in proportion as the black man, by reason of his skill, intelligence, and character, can produce something that the white man wants or respects in the commercial world. This is another reason why at Tuskegee we push the industrial training. We find that as every year we put into a Southern community colored men who can start a brick-yard, a sawmill, a tin-shop, or a printing-office,—men who produce something that makes the white man partly dependent upon the negro, instead of all the dependence being on the other side,—a change takes place in the relations of the races.

Let us go on for a few more years knitting our business and industrial relations into those of the white man, till a black man gets a mortgage on a white man's house that he can foreclose at will. The white man on whose house the mortgage rests will not try to prevent that negro from voting when he goes to the polls. It is through the dairy farm, the truck garden, the trades, and commercial life, largely, that the negro is to find his way to the enjoyment of all his rights. Whether he will or not, a white man respects a negro who owns a two-story brick house.

## REFLECTIVE ACTIVITIES

1. How does Washington's early life experiences contradict the intersection of the poverty and education argument in the 21st century?
2. Identify three quotes in the article that are important to you. Explain why these quotes are important and how you might apply them to education and leadership.

3. What are the differences between Washington's industrial training versus the vocational and community colleges?
4. What are the implications for critical pedagogy in this article?

Chapter Three

# The Education of Black Folk

## 1916

## W. E. B. Du Bois

One of the unsung advantages of democracy is that of being consistently and unblushingly illogical. No despot, for instance, with any regard for his reputation could possibly have treated the education of the American Negro in such perfectly contradictory ways as has been done in this republic.

Avoiding controversy by confining himself to the period preceding the Civil War, Dr. Woodson has set down calmly and methodically the facts concerning our attitude toward Negro education for some two hundred and forty years. It is one of those tales which introduce us to a world tragedy.

Imagine, for instance, the forefathers facing this problem of human training: Here are Negroes. They are slaves. They ought to be slaves. Consequently, they must be trained as slaves. Then enters the devil of illogic: they have immortal souls, consequently they must be trained as Christians. No sooner, however, is an attempt made to train them as Christians than, lo! they get some dangerous intelligence. Anxious search ensues for methods of training slaves in Christianity without making them intelligent. "Religion Without Letters," Mr. Woodson calls it.

Meantime, before the magic method is discovered, the sparks of undesired intelligence spread. Free Negroes, even slaves, begin to educate themselves. Schools start up here and there, and matters look really alarming. Some black leaders appear, in religion and even in revolt. About 1835 comes determined reaction. We have gone quite far enough, whisper the advocates of slavery, and their whispering is reinforced and strengthened by a new economic note, for the cotton kingdom is rising. The kingdoms of silk and wool are receding, the American slave is to become an economic foundation stone, a new industrial element. Down with education—up with slavery!

31

Religion must still be taught, to be sure, for properly taught it makes better slaves; but no reading and writing, no real training of intelligence.

There ensued a long and dismal fight in which education became a thing of midnight strategy, a stolen wonder. Even the free Negroes of the North suffered from the reactionary blows. They were swept out of the public schools even in the few places where once they had entered. They established their own weak little institutions with difficulty and amid threats. Still the work went on doggedly and persistently, and bolder whites helped. Who does not remember Beriah Green in New York, and Prudence Crandall and her Connecticut troubles?

Slowly separate institutions and separate colored school systems arose. Gradually down toward wartime some little education here and there was provided at public expense. Indeed, the whole tale shows that by being frankly illogical a democracy may do exactly the thing which it has started out not to do and never know the difference.

Practically everything that happened before the war has been reproduced in larger scale since the war. We trust Dr. Woodson will not forget to tell us this later story, even though it raises much discussion and bitter controversy. Here we have again Negroes. They are serfs. They ought to be kept "in their place." They must therefore be trained as serfs. The illogical devil appears: Negroes also have brains. Modern work needs brains. But if we educate Negroes to work they may get sense enough to want to vote and even to know how to vote. Therefore, "industrial" training without the training of intelligence—but this is a tale for another book. Meanwhile the author has written a book worthwhile. It is provided with ample references, an appendix of original documents, and a very complete bibliography.

## REFLECTIVE ACTIVITIES

1. What comments in this article imply that the education of Black people is a national security threat?
2. What does "religion without letters" mean to you as it relates to educators? Think about "religion without letters" in the context of oppression.
3. Identify and explain three quotes that stand out to you in this article. What are the implications for educators?

*Chapter Four*

# The Seat of the Trouble

*1933*

## Carter G. Woodson

The "educated Negroes" have the attitude of contempt toward their own people because in their own as well as in their mixed schools Negroes are taught to admire the Hebrew, the Greek, the Latin and the Teuton and to despise the African. Of the hundreds of Negro high schools recently examined by an expert in the United States Bureau of Education only eighteen offer a course taking up the history of the Negro, and in most of the Negro colleges and universities where the Negro is thought of, the race is studied only as a problem or dismissed as of little consequence. For example, an officer of a Negro university, thinking that an additional course on the Negro should be given there, called upon a Negro Doctor of Philosophy of the faculty to offer such work. He promptly informed the officer that he knew nothing about the Negro. He did not go to school to waste his time that way. He went to be educated in a system which dismisses the Negro as a nonentity.

At a Negro summer school two years ago, a white instructor gave a course on the Negro, using for his text a work which teaches that whites are superior to the Blacks. When asked by one of the students why he used such a textbook the instructor replied that he wanted them to get that point of view. Even schools for Negroes, then, are places where they must be convinced of their inferiority.

The thought of the inferiority of the Negro is drilled into him in almost every class he enters and in almost every book he studies. If he happens to leave school after he masters the fundamentals, before he finishes high school or reach[es] college, he will naturally escape some of this bias and may recover in time to be of service to his people.

Practically all of the successful Negroes in this country are of the uneducated type or of that of Negroes who have had no formal education at all. The large majority of the Negroes who have put on the finishing touches of our best colleges are all but worthless in the development of their people. If after leaving school they have the opportunity to give out to Negroes what traducers of the race would like to have it learn such persons may thereby earn a living at teaching or preaching what they have been taught but they never become a constructive force in the development of the race. The so-called school, then, becomes a questionable factor in the life of this despised people.

As another has well said, to handicap a student by teaching him that his black face is a curse and that his struggle to change his condition is hopeless is the worst sort of lynching. It kills one's aspirations and dooms him to vagabondage and crime. It is strange, then, that the friends of truth and the promoters of freedom have not risen up against the present propaganda in the schools and crushed it. This crusade is much more important than the anti-lynching movement, because there would be no lynching if it did not start in the schoolroom. Why not exploit, enslave, or exterminate a class that everybody is taught to regard as inferior?

To be more explicit we may go to the seat of the trouble. Our most widely known scholars have been trained in universities outside of the South. Northern and Western institutions, however, have had no time to deal with matters which concern the Negro especially. They must direct their attention to the problems of the majority of their constituents, and too often they have stimulated their prejudices by referring to the Negro as unworthy of consideration. Most of what these universities have offered as language, mathematics, and science may have served a good purpose, but much of what they have taught as economics, history, literature, religion and philosophy is propaganda and can't that involved a waste of time and misdirected the Negroes thus trained.

And even in the certitude of science or mathematics it has been unfortunate that the approach to the Negro has been borrowed from a "foreign" method. For example, the teaching of arithmetic in the fifth grade in a backward county in Mississippi should mean one thing in the Negro school and a decidedly different thing in the white school. The Negro children, as a rule, come from the homes of tenants and peons who have to migrate annually from plantation to plantation, looking for light which they have never seen. The children from the homes of white planters and merchants live permanently in the midst of calculations, family budgets, and the like, which enable them sometimes to learn more by contact than the Negro can acquire in school. Instead of teaching such Negro children less arithmetic, they should be taught much more of it than the white children, for the latter attend a graded school consolidated by free transportation when the Negroes go to one-room rented hovels to be taught without equipment and by incompetent teachers educated scarcely beyond the eighth grade.

In schools of theology Negroes are taught the interpretation of the Bible worked out by those who have justified segregation and winked at the economic debasement of the Negro sometimes almost to the point of starvation. Deriving their sense of right from this teaching, graduates of such schools can have no message to grip the people whom they have been ill trained to serve. Most of such mis-educated ministers, therefore, preach to benches while illiterate Negro preachers do the best they can in supplying the spiritual needs of the masses.

In the schools of business administration Negroes are trained exclusively in the psychology and economics of Wall Street and are, therefore, made to despise the opportunities to run ice wagons, push banana carts, and sell peanuts among their own people. Foreigners, who have not studied economics but have studied Negroes, take up this business and grow rich.

In schools of journalism Negroes are being taught how to edit such metropolitan dailies as the *Chicago Tribune* and the *New York Times*, which would hardly hire a Negro as a janitor; and when these graduates come to the Negro weeklies for employment they are not prepared to function in such establishments, which, to be successful, must be built upon accurate knowledge of the psychology and philosophy of the Negro.

When a Negro has finished his education in our schools, then, he has been equipped to begin the life of an Americanized or Europeanized white man, but before he steps from the threshold of his alma mater he is told by his teachers that he must go back to his own people from whom he has been estranged by a vision of ideals which in his disillusionment he will realize that he cannot attain. He goes forth to play his part in life, but he must be both social and bi-social at the same time. While he is a part of the body politic, he is in addition to this a member of a particular race to which he must restrict himself in all matters social. While serving his country he must serve within a special group. While being a good American, he must above all things be a "good Negro"; and to perform this definite function he must learn to stay in a "Negro's place."

For the arduous task of serving a race thus handicapped, however, the Negro graduate has had little or no training at all. The people whom he has been ordered to serve have been belittled by his teachers to the extent that he can hardly find delight in undertaking what his education has led him to think is impossible. Considering his race as blank in achievement, then, he sets out to stimulate their imitation of others. The performance is kept up a while; but, like any other effort at meaningless imitation, it results in failure.

Facing this undesirable result, the highly educated Negro often grows sour. He becomes too pessimistic to be a constructive force and usually develops into a chronic fault-finder or a complainant at the bar of public opinion. Often when he sees that the fault lies at the door of the white oppressor whom he is afraid to attack, he turns upon the pioneering Negro who is at work doing the best he can to extricate himself from an uncomfortable predicament.

In this effort to imitate, however, these "educated people" are sincere. They hope to make the Negro conform quickly to the standard of the whites and thus remove the pretext for the barriers between the races. They do not realize, however, that even if the Negroes do successfully imitate the whites, nothing new has thereby been accomplished. You simply have a larger number of persons doing what others have been doing. The unusual gifts of the race have not thereby been developed, and an unwilling world, therefore, continues to wonder what the Negro is good for.

These "educated" people, however, decry any such thing as race consciousness; and in some respects they are right. They do not like to hear such expressions as "Negro literature," "Negro poetry," "African art," or "thinking Black"; and, roughly speaking, we must concede that such things do not exist. These things did not figure in the courses which they pursued in school, and why should they? "Aren't we all Americans? Then, whatever is American is as much the heritage of the Negro as of any other group in this country."

The "highly educated" contend, moreover, that when the Negro emphasizes these things he invites racial discrimination by recognizing such differentness of the races. The thought that the Negro is one thing and the white man another is the stock-in-trade argument of the Caucasian to justify segregation. Why, then, should the Negro blame the white man for doing what he himself does?

These "highly educated" Negroes, however, fail to see that it is not the Negro who takes this position. The white man forces him to it, and to extricate himself from the Negro leader, he must so deal with the situation as to develop in the segregated group the power with which they can elevate themselves.

The differentness of races, moreover, is no evidence of superiority or of inferiority. This merely indicates that each race has certain gifts which the others do not possess. It is by the development of these gifts that every race must justify its right to exist.

## REFLECTIVE ACTIVITIES

1. What are the implications from Woodson's article regarding the politics of curriculum that stand out to you?
2. How does second-generation segregation (tracking, magnet programs in predominantly Black schools with majority White student popula-

tions, Advanced Placement and Gifted Programs with majority White) mirror Woodson's concept of inferiority being drilled into the minds of Black students?

3. Reflecting on your educational leadership preparation program: Did you take courses that would help you deconstruct whiteness or were your courses in educational leadership more about managing systems?

4. Did you get angry while reading this article? If so what might be contributing to your anger?

*Chapter Five*

# Intelligence, Education, Universal Knowledge and How to Get It

*1937*

Marcus Garvey

You must never stop learning. The world's greatest men and women were people who educated themselves outside of the university with all the knowledge that the university gives, as [and?] you have the opportunity of doing the same thing the university student does—read and study.

One must never stop reading. Read everything that you can that is of standard knowledge. Don't waste time reading trashy literature. That is to say, don't pay any attention to the ten cents novels, wild west stories and cheap sentimental books, but where there is a good plot and a good story in the form of a novel, read it. It is necessary to read it for the purpose of getting information on human nature. The idea is that personal experience is not enough for a human to get all the useful knowledge of life, because the individual life is too short, so we must feed on the experience of others. The literature we read should include the biography and autobiography of men and women who have accomplished greatness in their particular line. Whenever you can buy these books and own them and whilst you are reading them make pencil or pen notes of the striking sentences and paragraphs that you should like to remember, so that when you have to refer to the book for any thought that you would like to refresh your mind on, you will not have to read over the whole book.

You should also read the best poetry for inspiration. The standard poets have always been the most inspirational creators. From a good line of poetry, you may get the inspiration for the career of a life time. Many a great man and woman was first inspired by some attractive line or verse of poetry.

There are good poets and bad poets just like there are good novels and bad novels. Always select the best poets for your inspirational urge.

Read history incessantly until you master it. This means your own national history, the history of the world—social history, industrial history, and the history of the different sciences; but primarily the history of man. If you do not know what went on before you came here and what is happening at the time you live, but away from you, you will not know the world and will be ignorant of the world and mankind.

You can only make the best out of life by knowing and understanding it. To know, you must fall back on the intelligence of others who came before you and have left their records behind.

To be able to read intelligently, you must first be able to master the language of your country. To do this, you must be well acquainted with its grammar and the science of it. Every six months you should read over again the science of the language that you speak, so as not to forget its rules. People judge you by your writing and your speech. If you write badly and incorrectly they become prejudiced toward your intelligence, and if you speak badly and incorrectly those who hear you become disgusted and will not pay much attention to you but in their hearts laugh after you. A leader who is to teach men and present any fact of truth to man must first be learned in his subject.

Never write or speak on a subject you know nothing about, for there is always somebody who knows that particular subject to laugh at you or to ask you embarrassing questions that may make others laugh at you. You can know about any subject under the sun by reading about it. If you cannot bu[y] the books outright and own them, go to your public libraries and read them there or borrow them, or join some circulating library in your district or town, so as to get the use of these books. You should do that as you may refer to them for information.

You should read at least four hours a day. The best time to read is in the evening after you have retired from your work and after you have rested and before sleeping hours but do so before morning, so that during your sleeping hours what you have read may become subconscious, that is to say, planted in your memory. Never go to bed without doing some reading.

Never keep the constant company of anybody who doesn't know as much as you or isn't as educated as you, and from whom you cannot learn something or reciprocate your learning, especially if that person is illiterate or ignorant because constant association with such a person will unconsciously cause you to drift into the peculiar culture or ignorance of that person. Always try to associate with people from whom you can learn something. Contact with cultured persons and with books is the best companionship you can have and keep.

By reading good books you keep the company of the authors of the book or the subjects of the book when otherwise you could not meet them in the social contact of life. NEVER GO DOWN IN INTELLIGENCE to those who are below you, but if possible help to lift them up to you and always try to ascend to those who are above you and be their equal with the hope of being their master.

Continue always in the application of the thing you desire educationally, culturally, or otherwise, and never give up until you reach the objective—and you can reach the objective if others have done so before you, proving by their doing it that it is possible.

In your desire to accomplish greatness, you must first decide in your own mind in what direction you desire to seek that greatness, and when you have so decided in your own mind, work unceasingly toward it. The particular thing that you may want should be before you all the time, and whatsoever it takes to get it or make it possible should be undertaken. Use your faculties and persuasion to achieve all you set your mind on.

Try never to repeat yourself in any one discourse in saying the same thing over and over except when you are making new points, because repetition is tiresome and it annoys those who hear the repetition. Therefore, try to possess as much universal knowledge as possible through reading so as to be able to be free of repetition in trying to drive home a point.

No one is ever too old to learn. Therefore, you should take advantage of every educational facility. If you should hear of a great man or woman who is to lecture or speak in your town on any given subject and the person is an authority on the subject, always make time to go and hear him. This is what is meant by learning from others. You should learn the two sides to every story, so as to be able to properly debate a question and hold your grounds with the side that you support. If you only know one side of a story, you cannot argue intelligently nor effectively. As for instance, to combat communism, you must know about it, otherwise people will take advantage of you and win a victory over your ignorance.

Anything that you are going to challenge, you must first know about it, so as to be able to defeat it. The moment you are ignorant about anything the person who has the intelligence of that thing will defeat you. Therefore, get knowledge, get it quickly, get it studiously, but get it anyway.

Knowledge is power. When you know a thing and can hold your ground on that thing and win over your opponents on that thing, those who hear you learn to have confidence in you and will trust your ability.

Never, therefore, attempt anything without being able to protect yourself on it, for every time you are defeated it takes away from your prestige and you are not as respected as before.

All the knowledge you want is in the world, and all that you have to do is to go seeking it and never stop until you have found it. You can find knowledge or the information about it in the public libraries, if it is not on your own bookshelf. Try to have a book and own it on every bit of knowledge you want. You may generally get these books at second hand book stores for sometimes one-fifth of the original value.

Always have a well equipped shelf of books. Nearly all information about mankind is to be found in the Encyclopedia Britannica. This is an expensive set of books, but try to get them. Buy a complete edition for yourself, and keep it at your home, and whenever you are in doubt about anything, go to it and you will find it there.

The value of knowledge is to use it. It is not humanly possible that a person can retain all knowledge of the world, but if a person knows how to search for all the knowledge of the world, he will find it when he wants it.

A doctor or a lawyer although he passed his examination in college does not know all the laws and does not know all the techniques of medicine but he has the fundamental knowledge. When he wants a particular kind of knowledge, he goes to the medical books or law books and refers to the particular law or how to use the recipe of medicine. You must, therefore, know where to find your facts and use them as you want them. No one will know where you got them, but you will have the facts and by using the facts correctly they will think you a wonderful person, a great genius, and a trusted leader.

In reading it is not necessary or compulsory that you agree with every-thing you read. You must always use or apply your own reasoning to what you have read based upon what you already know as touching the facts on what you have read. Pass judgement on what you read based upon these facts. When I say facts I mean things that cannot be disputed. You may read thoughts that are old, and opinions that are old and have changed since they were written. You must always search to find out the latest facts on that particular subject and only when these facts are consistently maintained in what you read should you agree with them, otherwise you are entitled to your own opinion.

Always have up-to-date knowledge. You can gather this from the latest books and the latest periodicals, journals and newspapers. Read your daily newspaper everyday. Read a standard monthly journal every month, a stan-dard weekly magazine every week, a standard quarterly magazine every quarter and by this you will find the new knowledge of the whole year in addition to the books you read, whose facts have not altered in that year. Don't keep old ideas, bury them as new ones come.

## HOW TO READ

Use every spare minute you have in reading. If you are going on a journey that would take you an hour carry something with you to read for that hour until you have reached the place. If you are sitting down waiting for somebody, have something in your pocket to read until the person comes. Don't waste time. Any time you think you have to waste put it in reading something. Carry with you a small pocket dictionary and study words whilst waiting or travelling, or a small pocket volume on some particular subject. Read through at least one book every week separate and distinct from your newspapers and journals. It will mean that at the end of one year you will have read fifty-two different subjects. After five years you will have read over two hundred and fifty books. You may be considered then a well read man or a well read woman and there will be a great difference between you and the person who has not read one book. You will be considered intelligent and the other person be considered ignorant. You and that person therefore will be living in two different worlds; one the world of ignorance and the other the world of intelligence. Never forget that intelligence rules the world and ignorance carries the burden. Therefore, remove yourself as far as possible from ignorance and seek as far as possible to be intelligent.

Your language being English you should study the English language thoroughly. To know the English language thoroughly you ought to be acquainted with Latin, because most of the English words are of Latin origin. It is also advisable that you know the French language because most of the books that you read in English carry Latin and French phrases and words. There is no use reading a page or paragraph of a book or even a sentence without understanding it.

If it has foreign words in it, before you pass over them you should go to the dictionary, if you don't know the meaning and find out the meaning. Never pass over a word without knowing its meaning. The dictionary and the books on word building which can be secured from book sellers will help you greatly.

I know a boy who was ambitious to learn. He hadn't the opportunity of an early school education because he had to work ten hours a day, but he determined that he would learn and so he took with him to his work place every day a simplified grammar and he would read and memorize passages and the rules of grammar whilst at work.

After one year he was almost an expert in the grammar of his language. He knew the different parts of speech, he could paraphrase, analyze and construct sentences. He also took with him a pocket dictionary and he would write out twenty-five new words with their meanings every day and study these words and their forms and their meaning. After one year he had a speaking vocabulary of more than three thousand words. He continued this for several years and when he became a man he had a vocabulary at his command of over fifteen thousand words. He became an author because he could write in his language by having command of words. What he wrote was his experiences and he recorded his experiences in the best words of his language. He was not able to write properly at the same age and so he took with him to work what is called in school a copying book and he practiced the copying of letters until he was able to write a very good hand. He naturally became acquainted with literature and so he continued reading extensively. When he died he was one of the greatest scholars the world ever knew. Apply the story to yourself.

There is nothing in the world that you want that you cannot have so long as it is possible in nature and men have achieved it before. The greatest men and women in the world burn the midnight lamp. That is to say, when their neighbors and household are gone to bed, they are reading, studying and thinking. When they rise in the morning they are always ahead of their neighbors and their household in the thing that they were studying, reading and thinking of. A daily repetition of that will carry them daily ahead and above their neighbors and household. Practice this rule. It is wise to study a couple of subjects at a time. As for instance—a little geography, a little psychology, a little ethics, a little theology, a little philosophy, a little mathematics, a little science on which a sound academic education is built. Doing this week after week, month after month, year after year will make you so learned in the liberal arts as to make you ready and fit for your place in the affairs of the world. If you know what others do not know, they will want to hear you. You will then become invaluable in your community and to your country, because men and women will want to hear you and see you everywhere.

As stated before, books are one's best companions. Try to get them and keep them. A method of doing so is every time you have ten cents or twenty five cents or a dollar to spend foolishly, either on your friends or yourself, think how much more useful that ten or twenty five cents or dollar would be invested in a book and so invest it. It may be just the thing you have been looking for to give you a thought by which you may win the heart of the world. The ten cent, twenty five cent or a dollar, therefore, may turn out to be an investment of worth to the extent of a million dollars. Never lend anybody the book that you want. You will never get it back. Never allow anybody to go to your bookshelf in your absence because the very book that you may want most may be taken from the shelf and you may never be able to get one of the kind again.

If you have a library of your own, lock it when you are not at home. Spend most of your spare time in your library. If you have a radio keep it in your own library and use it exhaustively to listen to lectures, recitals, speeches and good music. You can learn a lot from the radio. You can be inspired a lot by good music [lines repeated]. Good music carries the sentiment of harmony and you may think many a good thought out of listening to good music.

Read a chapter from the Bible everyday, Old and New Testaments. The greatest wisdom of the age is to be found in the Scriptures. You can always quote from the Scriptures. It is the quickest way of winning approval.

## TRAGEDY OF WHITE INJUSTICE

1. Read and study thoroughly the poem "Tragedy of White Injustice" and apply its sentiment and statements in connection with the historic character and behavior of the white man. Know it so well as always to be able to be on guard against any professions of the white man in his suggested friendship for the Negro.

The poem exposes the white man's behavior in history and is intended to suggest distrust of him in every phase of life. Never allow it to get into the hands of a white man if possible.

2. You can improve your English as you go along by reading critically the books of the language; that is to say, you must pay close attention to the construction of sentences and paragraphs as you see them in the books you read. Imitate the style.

Read with observation. Never read carelessly and recklessly.

3. In reading books written by white authors of whatsoever kind, be aware of the fact that they are [not] written for your particular benefit or for the benefit of your race. They always write from their own point of view and only in the interest of their own race.

Never swallow wholly what the white man writes or says without first critically analyzing it and investigating it. The white man's trick is to deceive other people for his own benefit and profit.

Always be on your guard against him with whatsoever he does or says. Never take chances with him. His school books in the elementary schools, in the high schools, in the colleges and universities are all fixed up to suit his own purposes, to put him on top and keep him on top of other people. Don't trust him. Beware! Beware!

You should study carefully the subject of ethnology. It is the subject that causes races to know the difference between one race and another.

Ethnic relationship is important as it reveals the characteristic of one people as different from another. There is no doubt that each race has different habits and manners of behavior. You must know them so as to be able to deal with them. There are books on this subject in the library. In your reading and searching for truth always try to get that which is particularly helpful to the Negro. Every thought that strikes you, see how it fits in with the Negro, and to what extent you can use it to his benefit or in his behalf. Your entire obsession must be to see things from the Negro's point of view, remembering always that you are a Negro striving for Negro supremacy in every department of life, so that any truth you see or any facts you gather must be twisted to suit the Negro psychology of things.

The educational system of today hides the truth as far as the Negro is concerned. Therefore, you must searchingly scan everything you read particularly history, to see what you can pick out for the good of the race. As for instance, you will read that the Egyptians were a great people, the Carthagenians, the Libyans, etc., but you will not be told that they were black people or Negroes. You should, therefore, go beyond the mere statement of these events to discover the truth that will be creditable to your race. You would, therefore, in a case like that ask where did the Libyans get their civilization from or the Carthagenians or the Egyptians.

Following that kind of an investigation you will come upon the truth that it was all original Negro and subsequently became Negroid. That is to say, subsequent people were mixed with other people's blood, who were no doubt conquered by the Negro. As a fact, the original Egyptians were black men and women, and so the Carthagenians and Libyans, but in the later centuries they became mixed in blood, just as how now? the blacks are being mixed in America and the West Indies by the infusion of white blood through the domination of the white man.

Never yield to any statement in history or made by any individual, caring not how great, that the Negro was nobody in history. Even if you cannot prove it always claim that the Negro was great. Read everything you can get written by Negroes and their ancestry, going back six thousand years. There are statements in the Bible in the Old and New Testaments to show that black was always an important color among the races of men. Abraham had company with a black woman, even though he had his wife Sarah, by whom he had Ishmael.

All the original Pharaohs were black. Tutankumen, whose bones and body were dug up not very long ago at Luxor in Egypt, was a black Pharaoh. The sphinx, in Egypt which has stood through the millenniums, has black features. It is evident that as art it was portrayed to teach us of the greatness of men. When you are dealing with Jews let them know that they were once your slaves in Egypt if you have to say so. There is good ground to say that civilization started in Africa and passed from and through Northern Africa into Southern Europe, from which the Greeks and Romans and the People of Asia Minor made good copies. The swarthy color of the Asiatics and the brunette color of the South Europeans were due to the fact that the cultured and civilized blacks of Africa mixed their blood with them. Search all history and all literature and the Bible and find facts to support this argument but hold to it with a grip that will never loosen. Things that may not be true can be made if you repeat them long and often enough, therefore, always repeat statements that will give your race a status and an advantage. That is how the white man has built up his system of superiority. He is always telling you he is superior and he has written history and literature to prove it. You must do the same. One of the great backgrounds for your argument which cannot be disputed is that you are older than any other man as a race because you are black. Your argument is that in nature everything by way of age darkens. That you are darker than the rest of men, proves logically, that you are older than the rest of men. Another proof of that is that even among white people they grow darker in skin as they grow older in age in a lifetime.

If the one individual were to live for six thousand years he would surely be not white. If he were born white he would be as dark as the darkest man. Therefore, the old argument that the black man is black because as man he is older than the other man is good. Use it everywhere you go to defeat the white man in his belief that you sprung from something else. Use the argument that the white man is white because most of the time when the black man was great in Africa and had succeeded in running him across the Mediterranean into South Europe he had to hide himself in caves where there was very little light and air. He was almost covered up for most of the time in darkness. In natural creation the child in the womb of the mother is almost white even though it be a black child and it is almost born white and doesn't change color until it comes in contact with light and air.

Living in caves for so many centuries the white man, therefore, became colorless and the length of time always made it so that he was born naturally white. You must interpret anthropology to suit yourself. The thing for you to do is to refute every pertinent statement of the white man which tends to degrade you and to elevate him. Turn the tables on him and search for all reasons in the world you can find to justify it. That is how new thoughts are given out by creation. Never yield to the statement of your inferiority.

In reading Christian literature and accepting the doctrine of Jesus Christ lay special claim to your association with Jesus and the Son of God. Show that whilst the white and yellow worlds, that is to say—the worlds of Europe and Asia Minor persecuted and crucified Jesus the Son of God, it was the black race through Simon the black Cyrenian who befriended the Son of God and took up the Cross and bore it alongside of Him up to the heights of Calvary. The Roman Catholics, therefore, have no rightful claim to the Cross nor is any other professing Christian before the Negro. The Cross is the property of the Negro in his religion, because it was he who bore it.

Never admit that Jesus Christ was a white man, otherwise he could not be the Son of God and God to redeem all mankind. Jesus Christ had the blood of all races in his veins, and tracing the Jewish race back to Abraham and to Moses, from which Jesus sprang through the line of Jesse, you will find Negro blood everywhere, so Jesus had much of Negro blood in him.

Read the genealogical tree of Jesus in the Bible and you will learn from where he sprang. It is a fact that the white man has borrowed his civilization from other peoples. The first civilization was the Negro's—black people. The second civilization was the brown people—Indians, the third civilization was the yellow people, Chinese or Mongols; the last civilization up to today is the white man and all civilization goes back to the black man in the Nile Valley of Africa. In your reading, therefore, search for all these facts. Never stop reading and never stop until you find the proof of them.

You must pay great attention to sociology. Get the best books on the subject that you can and read them thoroughly. Find out the social relationship among other races so that you may know how to advise your people in their social behavior. Never admit that the Negro is more immoral than the white man but try to prove to the contrary. Socially the white man has debauched and debased all other races because of his dominant power. He is responsible for more illegitimacy among races than any other race. He has left bastard children everywhere he has been, therefore, he is not competent to say that he is socially and morally purer than any other race.

The mixed population among Neg[roe]s from slavery to the present in certain countries is due to [t]he white man's immorality. Therefore, if you should hear anyone talking about moral depravity of Negroes and the moral excellence of the whites, draw the above facts to their attention.

When through reading and research you have discovered any new fact helpful to the dignity and prestige, character and accomplishment of the Negro, always make a noise about it. You should keep always with you a note book and fountain pen or indelible pencil and make a note in that book of anything you hear or see that you would like to remember. Keep always at home a larger note book to which you must transfer the thought or experience, so that it will not be lost to your memory. Once at least every three months read over that book and as the book becomes more voluminous with facts, read it over at least once a year.

By the constant reading of these facts they will be planted on your subconscious mind and you will be able to use them without even knowing that you are doing so. By keeping your facts registered and your very important experiences, at the end of a full life you may have a volume of great value such as Elbert Hubbard's Scrap Book. Get a copy of this Scrap Book. Ask any publisher in your town to get it for you. It contains invaluable inspiration. Always have a thought. Make it always a beautiful thought. The world is attracted by beauty either in art or in expression. Therefore, try to read, think and speak beautiful things.

*Out of the night that covers me, Black as the Pit from pole to pole, I thank whatever Gods may be For my unconquerable soul. In the fell clutch of circumstance I have not winced nor cried aloud, Under the bludgeoning of chance My head is bloody, but unbowed. Beyond this place of wrath and tears Looms but the horror of the Shade, And yet the menace of the years Finds, and shall find, me unafraid. It matters not how strait the gate, How*

*charged with punishments the scroll, I am the master of my fate; I am the*
*captain of my soul. "INVICTUS" BY W. E. HENLEY*

## REFLECTIVE ACTIVITIES

1. Using four direct quotes identify what you think are important points in the article.
2. Reflecting on the study of history: How does Garvey's recommendation that Black students read as much as they can about their ancestry contradict what is taking place in 21st-century schools?
3. What are the implications of this article for curriculum and instructional leaders?
4. Contrary to Garvey's appeal for Blacks to read, how has high-stakes testing been used as a weapon to make students dislike reading?
5. How does Garvey's article contribute to critical White studies?

*Chapter Six*

# The Purpose of Education

*1947*

Dr. Martin Luther King Jr.

As I engage in the so-called "bull sessions" around and about the school, I too often find that most college men have a misconception of the purpose of education. Most of the "brethren" think that education should equip them with the proper instruments of exploitation so that they can forever trample over the masses. Still others think that education should furnish them with noble ends rather than means to an end.

It seems to me that education has a two-fold function to perform in the life of man and in society: the one is utility and the other is culture. Education must enable a man to become more efficient, to achieve with increasing facility the legitimate goals of his life.

Education must also train one for quick, resolute and effective thinking. To think incisively and to think for one's self is very difficult. We are prone to let our mental life become invaded by legions of half truths, prejudices, and propaganda. At this point, I often wonder whether or not education is fulfilling its purpose. A great majority of the so-called educated people do not think logically and scientifically. Even the press, the classroom, the platform, and the pulpit in many instances do not give us objective and unbiased truths. To save man from the morass of propaganda, in my opinion, is one of the chief aims of education. Education must enable one to sift and weigh evidence, to discern the true from the false, the real from the unreal, and the acts from the fiction.

The function of education, therefore, is to teach one to think intensively and to think critically. But education which stops with efficiency may prove the greatest menace to society. The most dangerous criminal may be the man gifted with reason, but with no morals. The late Eugene Talmadge, in my opinion, possessed one of the better minds of Georgia, or even America. Moreover, he wore the Phi Beta Kappa key. By all measuring rods, Mr. Talmadge could think critically and intensively; yet he contends that I am an inferior being. Are those the types of men we call educated?

We must remember that intelligence is not enough. Intelligence plus character—that is the goal of true education. The complete education gives one not only power of concentration, but worthy objectives upon which to concentrate. The broad education will, therefore, transmit to one not only the accumulated knowledge of the race but also the accumulated experience of social living.

If we are not careful, our colleges will produce a group of close-minded, unscientific, illogical propagandists, consumed with immoral acts. Be careful, "brethren!" Be careful, teachers!

## REFLECTIVE ACTIVITIES

1. How does Dr. King's article on the purpose of education contradict the current human capitalist ideology that is driving educational policy?
2. Identify at least three quotes that stand out to you and discuss why these points are important to you.

*Chapter Seven*

# A Talk to Teachers

*1963*

James Baldwin

Let's begin by saying that we are living through a very dangerous time. Everyone in this room is in one way or another aware of that. We are in a revolutionary situation, no matter how unpopular that word has become in this country. The society in which we live is desperately menaced, not by Khrushchev, but from within. To any citizen of this country who figures himself as responsible—and particularly those of you who deal with the minds and hearts of young people—must be prepared to "go for broke." Or to put it another way, you must understand that in the attempt to correct so many generations of bad faith and cruelty, when it is operating not only in the classroom but in society, you will meet the most fantastic, the most brutal, and the most determined resistance. There is no point in pretending that this won't happen.

Since I am talking to schoolteachers and I am not a teacher myself, and in some ways am fairly easily intimidated, I beg you to let me leave that and go back to what I think to be the entire purpose of education in the first place. It would seem to me that when a child is born, if I'm the child's parent, it is my obligation and my high duty to civilize that child. Man is a social animal. He cannot exist without a society. A society, in turn, depends on certain things which everyone within that society takes for granted. Now the crucial para-dox which confronts us here is that the whole process of education occurs within a social framework and is designed to perpetuate the aims of society. Thus, for example, the boys and girls who were born during the era of the Third Reich, when educated to the purposes of the Third Reich, became barbarians. The paradox of education is precisely this—that as one begins to become conscious one begins to examine the society in which he is being educated. The purpose of education, finally, is to create in a person the ability to look at the world for himself, to make his own decisions, to say to himself this is black or this is white, to decide for himself whether there is a God in heaven or not. To ask questions of the universe, and then learn to live with those questions, is the way he achieves his own identity. But no society is really anxious to have that kind of person around. What societies really, ideally, want is a citizenry which will simply obey the rules of society. If a society succeeds in this, that society is about to perish. The obligation of anyone who thinks of himself as responsible is to examine society and try to change it and to fight it—at no matter what risk. This is the only hope society has. This is the only way societies change.

Now, if what I have tried to sketch has any validity, it becomes thoroughly clear, at least to me, that any Negro who is born in this country and undergoes the American educational system runs the risk of becoming schizophrenic. On the one hand he is born in the shadow of the stars and stripes and he is assured it represents a nation which has never lost a war. He pledges allegiance to that flag which guarantees "liberty and justice for all." He is part of a country in which anyone can become president, and so forth. But on the other hand he is also assured by his country and his countrymen that he has never contributed anything to civilization—that his past is nothing more than a record of humiliations gladly endured. He is assumed by the republic that he, his father, his mother, and his ancestors were happy, shiftless, watermelon-eating darkies who loved Mr. Charlie and Miss Ann, that the value he has as a black man is proven by one thing only—his devotion to white people. If you think I am exaggerating, examine the myths which proliferate in this country about Negroes.

All this enters the child's consciousness much sooner than we as adults would like to think it does. As adults, we are easily fooled because we are so anxious to be fooled. But children are very different. Children, not yet aware that it is dangerous to look too deeply at anything, look at everything, look at each other, and draw their own conclusions. They don't have the vocabulary to express what they see, and we, their elders, know how to intimidate them very easily and very soon. But a black child, looking at the world around him, though he cannot know quite what to make of it, is aware that there is a reason why his mother works so hard, why his father is always on edge. He is aware that there is some reason why, if he sits down in the front of the bus, his father or mother slaps him and drags him to the back of the bus. He is aware that there is some terrible weight on his parents' shoulders which menaces him. And it isn't long—in fact it begins when he is in school— before he discovers the shape of his oppression.

Let us say that the child is seven years old and I am his father, and I decide to take him to the zoo, or to Madison Square Garden, or to the U.N. Building, or to any of the tremendous monuments we find all over New

York. We get into a bus and we go from where I live on 131st Street and Seventh Avenue downtown through the park and we get in New York City, which is not Harlem. Now, where the boy lives—even if it is a housing project—is in an undesirable neighborhood. If he lives in one of those housing projects of which everyone in New York is so proud, he has at the front door, if not closer, the pimps, the whores, the junkies—in a word, the danger of life in the ghetto. And the child knows this, though he doesn't know why.

I still remember my first sight of New York. It was really another city when I was born—where I was born. We looked down over the Park Avenue streetcar tracks. It was Park Avenue, but I didn't know what Park Avenue meant *downtown*. The Park Avenue I grew up on, which is still standing, is dark and dirty. No one would dream of opening a Tiffany's on that Park Avenue, and when you go downtown you discover that you are literally in the white world. It is rich—or at least it looks rich. It is clean—because they collect garbage downtown. There are doormen. People walk about as though they owned where they are—and indeed they do. And it's a great shock. It's very hard to relate yourself to this. You don't know what it means. You know—you know instinctively—that none of this is for you. You know this before you are told. And who is it for and who is paying for it? And why isn't it for you?

Later on when you become a grocery boy or messenger and you try to enter one of those buildings a man says, "Go to the back door." Still later, if you happen by some odd chance to have a friend in one of those buildings, the man says, "Where's your package?" Now this by no means is the core of the matter. What I'm trying to get at is that by the time the Negro child has had, effectively, almost all the doors of opportunity slammed in his face, and there are very few things he can do about it. He can more or less accept it with an absolutely inarticulate and dangerous rage inside—all the more dangerous because it is never expressed. It is precisely those silent people whom white people see every day of their lives—I mean your porter and your maid, who never say anything more than "Yes Sir" and "No, Ma'am." They will tell you it's raining if that is what you want to hear, and they will tell you the sun is shining if *that* is what you want to hear. They really hate you—really hate you because in their eyes (and they're right) you stand between them and life. I want to come back to that in a moment. It is the most sinister of the facts, I think, which we now face.

There is something else the Negro child can do, to[o]. Every street boy— and I was a street boy, so I know—looking at the society which has produced him, looking at the standards of that society which are not honored by anybody, looking at your churches and the government and the politicians, understand[s] that this structure is operated for someone else's benefit—not for his. And there's no reason in it for him. If he is really cunning, really ruthless, really strong—and many of us are—he becomes a kind of criminal.

He becomes a kind of criminal because that's the only way he can live. Harlem and every ghetto in this city—every ghetto in this country—is full of people who live outside the law. They wouldn't dream of calling a police-man. They wouldn't, for a moment, listen to any of those professions of which we are so proud on the Fourth of July. They have turned away from this country forever and totally. They live by their wits and really long to see the day when the entire structure comes down.

The point of all this is that black men were brought here as a source of cheap labor. They were indispensable to the economy. In order to justify the fact that men were treated as though they were animals, the white republic had to brainwash itself into believing that they were, indeed, animals and *deserved* to be treated like animals. Therefor[e] it is almost impossible for any Negro child to discover anything about his actual history. The reason is that this "animal," once he suspects his own worth, once he starts believing that he is a man, has begun to attack the entire power structure. This is why America has spent such a long time keeping the Negro in his place. What I am trying to suggest to you is that it was not an accident, it was not an act of God, it was not done by well-meaning people muddling into something which they didn't understand. It was a deliberate policy hammered into place in order to make money from black flesh. And now, in 1963, because we have never faced this fact, we are in intolerable trouble.

The Reconstruction, as I read the evidence, was a bargain between the North and South to this effect: "We've liberated them from the land—and delivered them to the bosses." When we left Mississippi to come North we did not come to freedom. We came to the bottom of the labor market, and we are still there. Even the Depression of the 1930's failed to make a dent in Negroes' relationship to white workers in the labor unions. Even today, so brainwashed is this republic that people seriously ask in what they suppose to be good faith, "What does the Negro want?" I've heard a great many asinine questions in my life, but that is perhaps the most asinine and perhaps the most insulting. But the point here is that people who ask that question, thinking that they ask it in good faith, are really the victims of this conspiracy to make Negroes believe they are less than human.

In order for me to live, I decided very early that some mistake had been made somewhere. I was not a "nigger" even though you called me one. But if I was a "nigger" in your eyes, there was something about *you*—there was something *you* needed. I had to realize when I was very young that I was none of those things I was told I was. I was not, for example, happy. I never touched a watermelon for all kinds of reasons that had been invented by white people, and I knew enough about life by this time to understand that whatever you invent, whatever you project, is you! So where we are no[w] is that a whole country of people believe I'm a "nigger," and I *don't*, and the battle's on! Because if I am not what I've been told I am, then it means that *you're* not what *you* thought you were *either*! And that is the crisis.

It is not really a "Negro revolution" that is upsetting the country. What is upsetting the country is a sense of its own identity. If, for example, one managed to change the curriculum in all the schools so that Negroes learned more about themselves and their real contributions to this culture, you would be liberating not only Negroes, you'd be liberating white people who know nothing about their own history. And the reason is that if you are compelled to lie about one aspect of anybody's history, you must lie about it all. If you have to lie about my real role here, if you have to pretend that I hoed all that cotton just because I loved you, then you have done something to yourself. You are mad.

Now let's go back a minute. I talked earlier about those silent people—the porter and the maid—who, as I said, don't look up at the sky if you ask them if it is raining, but look into your face. My ancestors and I were very well trained. We understood very early that this was not a Christian nation. It didn't matter what you said or how often you went to church. My father and my mother and my grandfather and my grandmother knew that Christians didn't act this way. It was a simple as that. And if that was so there was no point in dealing with white people in terms of their own moral professions, for they were not going to honor them. What one did was to turn away, smiling all the time, and tell white people what they wanted to hear. But people always accuse you of reckless talk when you say this.

All this means that there are in this country tremendous reservoirs of bitterness which have never been able to find an outlet, but may find an outlet soon. It means that well-meaning white liberals place themselves in great danger when they try to deal with Negroes as though they were missionaries. It means, in brief, that a great price is demanded to liberate all those silent people so that they can breathe for the first time and *tell* you what they think of you. And a price is demanded to liberate all those white children—some of them near forty—who have never grown up, and who never will grow up, because they have no sense of their identity.

What passes for identity in America is a series of myths about one's heroic ancestors. It's astounding to me, for example, that so many people really appear to believe that the country was founded by a band of heroes who wanted to be free. That happens not to be true. What happened was that some people left Europe because they couldn't stay there any longer and had to go someplace else to make it. That's all. They were hungry, they were poor, they were convicts. Those who were making it in England, for example, did not get on the *Mayflower*. That's how the country was settled. Not by Gary Cooper. Yet we have a whole race of people, a whole republic, who believe the myths to the point where even today they select political representatives, as far as I can tell, by how closely they resemble Gary Cooper.

Now this is dangerously infantile, and it shows in every level of national life. When I was living in Europe, for example, one of the worst revelations to me was the way Americans walked around Europe buying this and buying that and insulting everybody—not even out of malice, just because they didn't know any better. Well, that is the way they have always treated me. They weren't cruel; they just didn't know you were alive. They didn't know you had any feelings.

What I am trying to suggest here is that in the doing of all this for 100 years or more, it is the American white man who has long since lost his grip on reality. In some peculiar way, having created this myth about Negroes, and the myth about his own history, he created myths about the world so that, for example, he was astounded that some people could prefer Castro, astounded that there are people in the world who don't go into hiding when they hear the word "Communism," astounded that Communism is one of the realities of the twentieth century which we will not overcome by pretending that it does not exist. The political level in this country now, on the part of people who should know better, is abysmal.

The Bible says somewhere that where there is no vision the people perish. I don't think anyone can doubt that in this country today we are menaced— intolerably menaced—by a lack of vision.

It is inconceivable that a sovereign people should continue, as we do so abjectly, to say, "I can't do anything about it. It's the government." The government is the creation of the people. It is responsible to the people. And the people are responsible for it. No American has the right to allow the present government to say, when Negro children are being bombed and hosed and shot and beaten all over the Deep South, that there is nothing we can do about it. There must have been a day in this country's life when the bombing of the children in Sunday School would have created a public uproar and endangered the life of a Governor Wallace. It happened here and there was no public uproar.

I began by saying that one of the paradoxes of education was that precisely at the point when you begin to develop a conscience, you must find yourself at war with your society. It is your responsibility to change society if you think of yourself as an educated person. And on the basis of the evidence—the moral and political evidence—one is compelled to say that this is a backward society. Now if I were a teacher in this school, or any Negro school, and I was dealing with Negro children, who were in my care only a few hours of every day and would then return to their homes and to the streets, children who have an apprehension of their future which with every hour grows grimmer and darker, I would try to teach them—I would try to make them know—that those streets, those houses, those dangers, those agonies by which they are surrounded, are criminal. I would try to make each child know that these things are the result of a criminal conspiracy to destroy him. I would teach him that if he intends to get to be a man, he must at once decide that he is stronger than this conspiracy and that he must never make his peace with it. And that one of his weapons for refusing to make his peace with it and for destroying it depends on what he decides he is worth. I would teach him that there are currently very few standards in this country which are worth a man's respect. That it is up to him to change these standards for the sake of the life and the health of the country. I would suggest to him that the popular culture—as represented, for example, on television and in comic books and in movies—is based on fantasies created by very ill people, and he must be aware that these are fantasies that have nothing to do with reality. I would teach him that the press he reads is not as free as it says it is—and that he can do something about that, too. I would try to make him know that just as American history is longer, larger, more various, more beautiful and more terrible than anything anyone has ever said about it, so is the world larger, more daring, more beautiful and more terrible, but principally larger—and that it belongs to him. I would teach him that he doesn't have to be bound by the expediencies of any given administration, any given policy, any given morality; that he has the right and the necessity to examine everything. I would try to show him that one has not learned anything about Castro when one says, "He is a Communist." This is a way of his not learning something about Castro, something about Cuba, something, in time, about the world. I would suggest to him that he is living, at the moment, in an enormous province. America is not the world and if America is going to become a nation, she must find a way—and this child must help her to find a way to use the tremendous potential and tremendous energy which this child represents. If this country does not find a way to use that energy, it will be destroyed by that energy.

## REFLECTIVE ACTIVITIES

1. What are four key points that stand out to you in this article? Use direct quotes to support your position.
2. What are the implications of this article as it relates to Black labor and education?
3. How do Baldwin's arguments about popular culture and schooling compare with Black education in the twenty-first century?
4. Using Baldwin's arguments develop a Power Point presentation for a professional development workshop for teachers to address a contemporary problem in educating Black students.

*Chapter Eight*

# History Is a Weapon

*1963*

Malcolm X

And next month they'll come up to show you another trick. They'll come at you and me next month with this Negro History Week, they call it. This week comes around once every year. And during this one week they drown us with propaganda about Negro history in Georgia and Mississippi and Alabama. Never do they take us back across the water, back home. They take us down home, but they never give us a history of back home. They never give us enough information to let us know what we were doing before we ended up in Mississippi, Alabama, Georgia, Texas, and some of those other prison states. They give us the impression with Negro History Week that we were cotton pickers all of our lives. Cotton pickers, orange growers, mammies, and uncles for the white man in this country—this is our history when you talk in terms of Negro History Week. They might tell you about one or two people who took a peanut and made another white man rich. George Washington Carver—he was a scientist, but he died broke. He made Ford rich. So he wasn't doing anything for himself and his people. He got a good name for us, but what did we get out of it? Nothing. The master got it.

Just like a dog who runs out in the woods and grabs a rabbit. No matter how hungry the dog is, does he eat it? No, he takes it back and lays it at the boss's feet. The boss skins it, takes the meat, and gives the dog the bones. And the dog is going right on, hungry again. But he could have gotten the rabbit and eaten it for himself. And [the] boss couldn't even have caught him until later, because he can outrun the boss.

It's the same way with you and me. Every contribution we make, we don't make it for our people, we make it for the man, we make it for our master. He gets the benefit from it. We die, not for our people, we die for

61

him. We don't die for our home and our house, we die for his house. We don't die for our country, we die for his country. A lot of you all were fools on the front lines, were you not? Yes, you were. You put on the uniform and went right up on the front lines like a roaring hound dog barking for master. And when you come back here—you've had to bark since you came back.

So Negro History Week reminds us of this. It doesn't remind us of past achievements, it reminds us only of the achievements we made in the Western Hemisphere under the tutelage of the white man. So that whatever achievement that was made in the Western Hemisphere that the spotlight is put upon, this is the white man's shrewd way of taking credit for whatever we have accomplished. But he never lets us know of an accomplishment that we made prior to being born here. This is another trick.

The worst trick of all is when he names us Negro and calls us Negro. And when we call ourselves that, we end up tricking ourselves. My brother Cassius Clay was on the screen the other night talking with Les Crane about the word *Negro*. I wish he wouldn't have gone so fast, because he was in a position to have done a very good job. But he was right in saying that we're not Negroes, and have never been, until we were brought here and made into that. We were scientifically produced by the white man. Whenever you see somebody who calls himself a Negro, he's a product of Western civilization —not only Western civilization, but Western crime. The Negro, as he is called or calls himself in the West, is the best evidence that can be used against Western civilization today.

One of the main reasons we are called Negro is so we won't know who we really are. And when you call yourself that, you don't know who you really are. You don't know what you are, you don't know where you came from, you don't know what is yours. As long as you call yourself a Negro, nothing is yours. No languages—you can't lay claim to any language, not even English; you mess it up. You can't lay claim to any name, any type of name, that will identify you as something that you should be. You can't lay claim to any culture as long as you use the word *Negro* to identify yourself. It attaches you to nothing. It doesn't even identify your color.

If you talk about one of them, they call themselves white, don't they? Or they might call someone else Puerto Rican to identify them. Mind you how they do this. When they call him a Puerto Rican, they're giving him a better name. Because there is a place called Puerto Rico, you know. It at least lets you know where he came from. So they'll say whites, Puerto Ricans, and Negroes. Pick up on that. That's a drag, brothers.

White is legitimate. It means that's what color they are. Puerto Rican tells you that they're something else, came from somewhere else, but they're here now. Negro doesn't tell you anything. I mean nothing, absolutely nothing. What do you identify it with? Tell me. Nothing. What do you attach it to, what do you attach to it? Nothing. It's completely in the middle of nowhere.

And when you call yourself that, that's where you are—right in the middle of nowhere. It doesn't give you a language, because there is no such thing as a Negro language. It doesn't give you a country, because there is no such thing as a Negro country. It doesn't give you a culture—there is no such thing as a Negro culture, it doesn't exist. The land doesn't exist, the culture doesn't exist, the language doesn't exist, and the man doesn't exist. They take you out of existence by calling you a Negro. And you can walk around in front of them all day long and they act like they don't even see you. Because you made yourself nonexistent. It's a person who has no history; and by having no history, he has no culture.

Just as a tree without roots is dead, a people without history or cultural roots also becomes a dead people. And when you look at us, those of us who are called Negro, we're called that because we are like a dead people. We have nothing to identify ourselves as part of the human family. You know, you take a tree, you can tell what kind of tree it is by looking at the leaves. If the leaves are gone, you can look at the bark and tell what kind it is. But when you find a tree with the leaves gone and the bark gone, everything gone, you call that a what? A stump. And you can't identify a stump as easily as you can identify a tree.

And this is the position that you and I are in here in America. Formerly we could be identified by the names we wore when we came here. When we were first brought here, we had different names. When we were first brought here, we had a different language. And these names and this language identified the culture that we were brought from, the land that we were brought from. In identifying that, we were able to point towards what we had produced, our net worth. But once our names were taken and our language was taken and our identity was destroyed and our roots were cut off with no history, we became like a stump, something dead, a twig over here in the Western Hemisphere. Anybody could step on us, trample upon us, or burn us, and there would be nothing that we could do about it.

Those of you who are religious, who go to church, know there are stories in the Bible that can be used easily to pretty well tell the condition of the Black man in America once he became a Negro. They refer to him in there as the lost sheep, meaning someone who is lost from his own kind, which is how you and I have been for the past four hundred years. We have been in a land where we are not citizens, or in a land where they have treated us as strangers.

They have another symbolic story in there, called the dry bones. Many of you have gone to church Sunday after Sunday and got, you know, the ghost, they call it—got happy. When the old preacher started singing about dry bones, you'd knock over benches, just because he was singing about those bones, "them dry bones"—I know how they say it. But you never could identify the symbolic meaning of those bones—how they were dead because they had been cut off from their own kind.

Our people here in America have been in the same condition as those dry bones that you sit in church singing about. But you shed more tears over those dry bones than you shed over yourself. This is a strange thing, but it shows what happens to a people when they are cut off and stripped of everything, like you and I have been cut off and stripped of everything. We become a people like no other people, and we are a people like no other people, there's no other people on earth like you and me. We're unique, we're different. They say that we're Negro, and they say that *Negro* means black; yet they don't call all Black people Negroes. You see the contradiction? Mind you, they say that we're Negro, because *Negro* means black in Spanish, yet they don't call all Black people Negroes. Something there doesn't add up.

And then to get around it they say mankind is divided up into three categories—Mongoloid, Caucasoid, and Negroid. Now pick up on that. And all Black people aren't Negroid—they've got some jet black ones that they classify as Caucasoid. But if you'll study very closely, all of the black ones that they classify as Caucasoid are those that still have great civilizations, or still have the remains of what was once a great civilization. The only ones that they classify as Negroid are those that they find with no evidence that they were ever civilized; then they call them Negroid. But they can't afford to let any black-skinned people who have evidence that they formerly occupied a high seat in civilization, they can't afford to let them be called Negroid, so they take them on into the Caucasoid classification.

And actually Caucasoid, Mongoloid, and Negroid—there's no such thing. These are so-called anthropological terms that were put together by anthropologists who were nothing but agents of the colonial powers, and they were purposely given that status, they were purposely given such scientific positions, in order that they could come up with definitions that would justify the European domination over the Africans and the Asians. So immediately they invented classifications that would automatically demote these people or put them on a lesser level. All of the Caucasoids are on a high level, the Negroids are kept at a low level. This is just plain trickery that their scientists engage in in order to keep you and me thinking that we never were anything, and therefore he's doing us a favor as he lets us step upward or forward in his particular society or civilization. I hope you understand what I am saying.

## REFLECTIVE ACTIVITIES

1.  Observation: Based on your observation in schools, does history have a prominence in the curriculum?

2. As an educational leader, what are the implications in this article for stimulating the thinking of Black students?
3. Identify four main points in the article that you think are significant.
4. Based on Malcolm's article, develop a Power Point that outlines your vision for infusing Black history into the school curriculum.

*Chapter Nine*

# Get Knowledge to Benefit Self

*1965*

Elijah Muhammad

I am for the acquiring of knowledge or the accumulating of knowledge—as we now call it; education. First, my people must be taught the knowledge of self. Then and only then will they be able to understand others and that which surrounds them. Anyone who does not have a knowledge of self is considered a victim of either amnesia or unconsciousness and is not very competent. The lack of knowledge of self is a prevailing condition among my people here in America. Gaining the knowledge of self makes us unite into a great unity. Knowledge of self makes you take on the great virtue of learning.

Many people have attempted to belittle or degrade my followers by referring to them as unlettered or unschooled. They do this to imply that the believers in Islam are ignorant. If such a claim were so, then all the more credit should be given for our striving for self-elevation with so little. But truth represents itself and stands for itself. No followers, nor any other people are more zealous about the acquiring of knowledge than my followers. Throughout the Holy Qur'an, the duty of a Muslim to acquire knowledge is spelled out.

My people should get an education which will benefit their own people and not an education adding to the "storehouse" of their teacher. We need education, but an education which removes us from the shackles of slavery and servitude. Get an education, but not an education which leaves us in an inferior position and without a future. Get an education, but not an education that leaves us looking to the slave-master for a job.

Education for my people should be where our children are off to themselves for the first 15 or 16 years in classes separated by sex. Then they could and should seek higher education without the danger of losing respect for self or seeking to lose their identity. No people strive to lose themselves among other people except the so-called American Negroes. This they do because of lack of knowledge of self.

We should acquire an education where our people will become better students than their teachers. Get an education which will make our people produce jobs for self and will make our people willing and able to go and do for self. Is this not the goal and aim of the many foreign students who are studying in this country? Will not these students return to their own nations and give their people the benefit of their learning? Did not Nkrumah return to Ghana to lead his people to independence with the benefit of learning he acquired here in America and elsewhere? Did not Dr. Hastings Banda return to give the benefit of his education to his people who are striving toward freedom and independence in Nyasaland? Did not Nnamdi Azikiwe of Nigeria give the benefit of his education to the upliftment and independence of his people. Does not America offer exchange scholarships to smaller, weaker and dependent foreign governments so their students will acquire knowledge to aid the people of those countries? Then why shouldn't the goal in education be the same for you and me? Why is scorn and abuse directed toward my followers and myself when we say our people should get an education which will aid, benefit and uplift our people? Any other people would consider it a lasting insult, of the worst type, to ask them to refrain from helping their people to be independent by contributing the benefit of their knowledge.

Get an education, but one which will instill the idea and desire to get something of your own, a country of your own and jobs of your own.

I recall, in 1922 or 1923, when a debate was taking place in Congress concerning appropriation of funds for Howard University, a school set aside to train my people, in the nation's capital. A senator said this, and it is in the records to be examined in effect: What would be the need of the government appropriating money to educate Negroes? He said that they would not teach our people the science of modern warfare (defense), birth control or chemistry. He knew these were things free people must know in order to protect, preserve and advance themselves. We have not been able to protect, preserve and advance ourselves. This shows the slave-master has been very successful in dominating us with an education beneficial to him. There is a saying among us, "Mother may have, father may have, but God blesses the child who has its own." It is time we had our own.

I want an education for my people that will let them exercise the right of freedom. We are 100 years up from slavery. We are constantly told that we are free. Why can't we take advantage of that freedom? I want an education for my people that will elevate them. Why should we always be lying at the gate begging for bread, shelter, clothing and jobs if we are free and educated? Do not get an education just to set it up as some useless symbolic monument to the Black man in the Western Hemisphere. We need an education that eliminates division among us. Acquire an education that creates unity and makes us desire to be with our own.

The acquiring of knowledge for our children and ourselves must not be limited to the three R's—reading, 'riting and 'rithmetic. It should instead include the history of the Black nation, the knowledge of civilization of man and the universe and all sciences. It will make us a greater people of tomorrow.

We must instill within our people the desire to learn and then use that learning for self. We must be obsessed with getting the type of education we may use toward the elevation and benefit of our people—when we have such people among us, we must make it possible for them to acquire this wealth which will be beneficial and useful to us.

One of the attributes of Allah, The All-Wise God, Who is the Supreme Being, is knowledge. Knowledge is the result of learning and is a force or energy that makes its bearer accomplish or overcome obstacles, barriers and resistance. In fact, God means possessor of power and force. The education my people need is that knowledge, the attribute of God, which creates power to accomplish and make progress in the good things or the righteous things. We have tried other means and ways and have failed. Why not try Islam? It is our only salvation. It is the religion of Allah, His prophets and our forefathers.

## REFLECTIVE ACTIVITIES

1. What do you think Muhammad means by knowledge of self and do you think schools teach Black students this knowledge?
2. What direct quotes in this article speak to the concept of critical pedagogy?
3. What would educational achievement look like under the educational ideas of Elijah Muhammad?
4. What does it mean to be educated in the science of warfare and mating?
5. Deconstruct Elijah Muhammad's definition of knowledge and apply it to educational practice in predominantly Black schools.

# Index

# About the Editor

**Abul Pitre** is professor and department chair in the Department of Educational Leadership and School Administration at Fayetteville State University. He was appointed as Edinboro University's first named professor for his work in African American education and held the distinguished title of the Carter G. Woodson Professor of Education.

# About the Writers

**James Baldwin** is known for his novels and activism. He was born in New York but eventually traveled south to cover the Civil Rights movement. During his travels he befriended the likes of Malcolm X and Martin Luther King Jr. His book *The Fire Next Time* and the documentary *I Am Not Your Negro* provide examples of his social justice activism.

**Frederick Douglass** was a leading spokesman in the abolitionist movement. After escaping from slavery Douglass taught himself to read and write. He critiqued American idealism and his famous speech *What to a Slave Is the Fourth of July* is powerful testament to the Africana critical theory tradition. In 1845 he published his autobiography, *Narrative of the Life of Frederick Douglass, an American Slave*.

**W.E.B. Du Bois** was a founder of the National Association for the Advancement of Colored People. In 1895, he became the first African American to receive a doctorate from Harvard University. A prolific writer, his book *The Souls of Black Folk* addresses many of the contemporary problems in American life. His thesis on the color line and his critique of whiteness are examples of his foresight.

**Marcus Garvey** was born in Jamaica but later moved to New York where in 1917 he established a branch of his United Negro Improvement Association. Garvey sought the unification of Black people throughout the world and to his credit published *The Negro World*. He was an avid reader who could speak on a wide range of topics. Garvey's contributions continue to speak to Black peoples' struggle for equal justice.

**Martin Luther King Jr.** was a civil rights leader. He received undergraduate degrees from Morehouse College and Crozer Theological Seminary. In 1955, he received his doctoral degree in systematic theology from Boston College. A major highlight in his illustrious leadership was the March on Washington in 1963 where he delivered the *I Have A Dream* speech. His last speech *I Have Been to The Mountaintop* was delivered the day before his assassination.

**Elijah Muhammad** best known by his followers as the Messenger of Allah is the patriarch of the Nation of Islam. Born Elijah Poole in the 1930s, he migrated from Sandersville, Georgia, to Detroit, Michigan, where he met Wallace D. Fard, the founder of the Nation of Islam. After Fard's departure in the 1930s he became the leader of the Nation of Islam establishing schools, temples, and a wide range of businesses. His widely read book *Message to the Blackman in America* continues to be a hallmark in the 21st century.

**Booker T. Washington** was born during slavery and later became one of the leading voices on Black education. He developed Tuskegee Institute (University) through the support of wealthy philanthropists. In 1895, his *Atlanta Compromise* speech sparked controversy causing many to say that it accommodated Whites. Washington is credited with writing forty-one books and his autobiography of *Up From Slavery* provides a foundation for understanding many of his views about education and politics.

**Carter G. Woodson** is best known as the father of Black History. In 1912, he earned his doctorate degree in history from Harvard University. He founded The Association for the Study of African American Life and History and *The Journal of Negro History*. His book *The Mis-Education of the Negro* is a classic book that continues to resonate in the 21st century.

**Malcolm X** attended school in Omaha, Nebraska. Disgruntled by a racist school experience he dropped out of school in the eighth grade and later became involved in criminal activities. He was arrested for larceny in 1946 and while in prison was introduced to the teachings of Elijah Muhammad. After his release from prison Elijah Muhammad appointed him as his national spokesperson. His speeches like the "Ballot or the Bullet" and "History is a Weapon" electrified his audiences.

Lightning Source UK Ltd.
Milton Keynes UK
UKHW011118201219
355666UK00008B/63/P